100 years of Childhood Innocence

Compiled by

ELIZABETH WILLIAMS

Sold in aid of ChildLine (helpline for children and young people based in UK)

In memory of my darling husband Gwyn Williams, always a child at heart; gone now but forever young. To Mary and especially Nell; to my family and also with love and very special thanks to those people who gave me their personal stories. Thank you to my Grandchildren and Great Nieces who have given me so much joy.

(Front cover - Paige Brown)

Back cover – Paige Brown; photo of

Cody, 5 days old with Nanny Libby, much

older

CONTENTS

Introduction

1900-1920

- Down Memory Lane with Nell
- Dad
- Chicken Pox
- Rainy Day
- Below Stairs
- Rochester Bridge
- Annie Remembers

1920-1940

- Memories from Muriel
- Doreen Delights Us
- Mary's Memories
- Alice's Words
- Laura from Menai Straits
- Cousin Bette
- No-one told me

1940s

- Thomas & Ida Hewett and their daughter Maureen
  (With a touch of World War 2)
- Peanuts
- Mum
- Violets
- Electricity
- From Sheelagh Clarke – a memory of May 1946 growing up in Church Road, Ballybunion, Co Kerry, Eire
- Lina
- Gillian Recalls
- Uncle Jack

1950s

- Smells of the Past
- Food Glorious Food
- Christmas
- Seaside
- Past Eight O'clock
- How Embarrassing
- At Risk
- Spoiled Brats
- You've Been Framed
- Soul to Sole
- Sharing
- Virgin Thoughts
- Jaw Breakers
- Modesty
- Carlotta from Canada

1960s

- Let us pray
- Here comes the Bride
- Christopher (1969)

1970s

- Eyes of a Child
- Sticky Story
- Next Please
- Newborn
- PC
- Fiona

1980s

- Arm in Arm
- Rabbits
- Acceptable
- Hillsborough
- Another Sticky Tale
- Angelic
- Wicked Mother?
- Un deux trois
- By the Sea
- Janni
- Carole
- Alison's Adventures

1990s

- Old Jim
- Jim
- Santa
- Reading Age?
- Old Barbie Doll
- Concepts
- Baa Baa
- Terrible Twos
- The Farm
- 2 Years, My experience

2000s

- Dane from Chile
- Rayen from Chile
- Special Eyes
- Must Try Harder
- More Prayers
- Ashes to Ashes
- In-between
- Bullied
- Dog's Breakfast
- Lost Property
- Money, money, money
- Song of Life
- What a View!
- Wearing Well
- Teacher Said
- When I grow up
- How to Explain
- Compliment
- Coming and Going
- Enchanting
- Off with her Head!
- Peace but when
- SuperGran
- Out of the mouths
- Depths
- Comical
- Disco
- Blasphemy

- Vocabulary
- **Regrets and Difficulties**
- Photographs
- **Quotations**

INTRODUCTION

Love of and from children is the greatest blessing. There are many children throughout the world who have neither love nor blessings. I was truly loved and blessed as a child and doubly blessed as a mother and grandmother. Some of these are accounts of my childhood, now in the last century. Other stories are from my family, children and grandchildren. There are anecdotes from people throughout the world whom I have been privileged to meet and accounts of childhood from opposing sides in the Second World War. Extreme poverty features in other descriptions and in contrast, brighter tales full of laughter and joy.

The narrative starts with Nell who was born in Wales in 1900 and ends with snippets of vocabulary from the youngest contributors, some born towards the end of the last century and four born in the new Millennium. Some of these are Nell's great-grandchildren.

The history does not end with this book but new history is beginning today.

Perhaps you don't have children or grandchildren; I hope then that these tales will evoke memories of your childhood.

Please share the joys and tears.

1900s

I met Nell in 1984, she was 84 years of age and very ill. She was in Benllech on Anglesey; she was beautiful. I wondered if I would see her again. She became my Mother-in-law and friend and was with us in London until she died in her 97th year.

1900-1920

DOWN MEMORY LANE WITH NEL

I was born in 1900, Bangor City, North Wales in a terraced house in Tabernacle Street. My parents were very young, my father 21 and my mother 18 and Dad was a Printer's compositor on a paper called the 'Weekly News'. I have a faint memory of being in a pram, dark green with a thin yellow line following its outline – no hood and no buoyancy.

We moved to Conwy and I remember starting school, feeling like a queen. My mother had ironed a marvellous green sash to put on my dress. It was a beautiful shade of green with a fringe. She tied it into a huge bow on my bottom and I entered a large hall, joining a long crocodile of children marching to music played on a piano. I think I was six. No-one ever took me to or collected me from school so it must have been safe for children in those days. My chief occupation was cutting out pictures from the papers and books; no playmates but quite happy with my scissors and my thoughts.

There are many things of historical interest in Conwy. The castle built by Edward I to keep the Welsh rebels in their proper place.

There were many bloody battles in the mountains, the only place the King failed to conquer. He had to build stone castles to keep himself safe. Those who build castles become prisoners themselves within them; it is the rebels who are free to roam the mountains.

This castle is now a tourist attraction. One day I stood by the rocky slope at Mount Pleasant and saw two dray horses pulling a wagon with our furniture in it, sparks flashing from the horses' hooves as they slithered and slipped on the flinty surface. We were moving back to Bangor.

At school girls learned knitting and sewing and I learned to read and write in both Welsh and English. We played all kinds of games – skipping; spinning tops; marbles; hoops; Jack Stones (wooden for the girls and iron for the boys). There were several popular singing games such as 'Puss Puss in the corner', 'Here we come gathering nuts in May', 'Wall flowers, wall flowers growing up so high', 'Round and round the Mulberry bush', 'In and out the windows' and 'Blind Man's Buff'. We also played Tag and sometimes dressed up playing weddings and funerals. If it rained we went into a cave-like place underneath St Paul's Infant school.

There was great poverty in Bangor at that time. I have one sad memory when I was eight years old. We had to recite our tables every day in sing song fashion. One day teacher gave everyone but me a tables' book. This did not bother me as I knew them all by heart. When she found me saying them without the book she went berserk and gave me the best beating I ever had in my life, the only one I ever had. My sister went home and told my parents who came straight to the school. The teacher denied everything and made the rest of my school year sheer hell. Every day I prayed for deliverance from her daring me to go home and tell my father of this or that.

At the beginning of each day the teacher put the date on the right hand corner of the blackboard and we copied it on to our slates. We later used copy books with scratchy nibs and ink. We had got used to saying 'nineteen o seven, nineteen o eight and nineteen o nine'. When the year changed to 1910, we all insisted on saying 'nineteen o ten' and it took ages for us to get used to not saying it this way. Remember here that this was 1910; my friend seemed to realise how near we were to a new century and wondered what we would call it. (When Nell wrote these words it was the 1990s.)

I can remember my father coming into my bedroom early one morning when he returned from night work and telling me that King Edward VII was dead; we were excited because we knew before the papers were printed. The whole town went into mourning with all the windows draped in either black or deep purple velvet.

Something that stands out in my memory is the sinking of the Titanic. My father took my sister and me to the big Tabernacle Chapel where a memorial service was held. The words are forgotten and although it was a very sad occasion, I often recall enjoying the sound of hundreds of voices singing 'Nearer my God to Thee'. Whenever I heard it in the future I always remembered the Titanic.

Nell's written memories of her family are kept for just her family but one piece stands out from the rest.

My eldest Aunt was a tailoress and in great demand especially in the making of tailored costumes and suits. As I grew older I was much attracted to her workrooms and became useful; at first, just picking up the pins on the floor, later taking out the tackings after the seams had been stitched.

I became familiar with all facets of dressmaking and while still under 10, I would buy a wooden Dutch doll from the shop next door. There were two sizes of doll, large for 2d and small 1d. For these I begged scraps of odd materials from my aunt and would devise wonderful (to me) clothes for these dolls after studying her Weldon's Fashion Books. There was no interest in my mind about nursing these dolls – I only wanted to clothe them. There were always some girls who came to learn the trade with her but I heard her say many times that I was better than any of them. My father and she had many arguments about this; she would have wished me to become what she called a court dressmaker by going to a London Fashion House but my Dad was adamant. I was to be a teacher.

Nell goes on to talk a lot of her childhood in Bangor.

Our landlord was Lord Penrhyn – he owned a very large estate and lived in a Castle a couple of miles away. He owned most of the houses around, the quarry where the slates were produced and a fleet of ships as well as the little railway line connecting the quarry with the port.

There were several ships in his fleet; we became used to hearing sounds from these sometimes at night when sailors would whistle or pipe to their families that they had arrived.

My favourite ship of all was different – it belonged to the days of sailing – she was called Mary B Mitchell and she was a three-masted schooner. When she came into the harbour, we as children often ran to see her at close quarters. We could do this because she sailed by the wind and had to make a right-about turn in the bay in order to get into port. This meant that all her sails would be blown to their full extent and the sight of this old lady in full sail was something I can never forget. I seem to have heard that she was sunk during the First World War. One of the other vessels was sunk by a German submarine early on in the War with the whole crew being saved by the German crew. This did not happen later when feelings on both sides became bitter. One night when I was in the chip shop (a new innovation to our way of life) the youngest crew member aged 14 told us of his adventure and how kind the enemy had been to him and his mates.

During school holidays we played on the beach, a terrible place that had been formed by dumping waste slate from a nearby yard where slates were dressed and polished to make grand fire-places, baths and billiard tables. Later the slates became covered in poor quality grass allowing boys to play football, whilst the girls became architects and built small houses with the larger pieces of slate. There was always plenty of rubbish in the way of pretty bits of glass and pottery to decorate these wonderful homes of our fancy. At certain times of the year eels appeared in their billions. At a place called 'Under the Rocks' where the river enters the sea by the port, the boys formed wool balls around pieces of meat or snails, leaving a long tail of the wool hanging and dropping the ball into the water. The young eels clung to the ball by their teeth and the boys would then jerk the end of the wool and scatter the eels all over the girls.

There was a wreck of an old hospital ship left on the beach – it was a wonderful piece of equipment, a relic of the days when typhoid fever was rampant in Bangor. (It was alluded to as the 'Bangor Disease' – 'cluy Bangor'.) Many people of my parents' generation and even older had pock-marked skins which meant they had survived an attack of typhus.

The hospital ship was built with a yellow flag hoisted to its mast and took the sufferers out to sea. This was the wrecked ship we played in, a second one being built. Typhus was beaten by inoculation and the laying of drains large enough to carry the waste and rain water clear of the town.

As the population grew, more and much larger drains were essential. Almost every summer until the twenties, the area in which I lived was flooded at every flood tide. High tides and heavy rains were too much for the existing drains and we had to evacuate the ground floor and live upstairs pro tem. Bread and milk were handed by means of long poles through the bedroom windows. Students of the Varsity and Normal College, who lodged in private houses, had to go in boats to colleges which were built on high ground. My mother was distraught when these disasters overtook us; she was very house-proud and broken-hearted when she contemplated the mess that was left behind. Everything was covered in mud; all the floors in need of new coverings, mostly lino and rugs which were hastily snatched up to a dry place. As soon as August passed, things fell back into place once more.

I had missed a lot of schooling as I had been very ill but was entered for the much sought after scholarship. This was in fact a bursary enabling the winners to have three years free education at the County School, in my case for Girls. Boys went to the Boys Friar's School, an ancient Grammar School dating from the days when Bangor boasted a Friary. The original school overlooked a field where the local football team played. During the First World War it was turned into allotments and football matches transferred to Farrar Road, not far from school.

Later the ruins of the old Friar's School became too handy for those who wished to have a free viewing of the football games so it was razed to the ground in case of accidents. The surrounding fields, now full of houses, then were full of cows.

Sadly because of the missed schooling I did not get a place in 1912 but was lucky enough to do so in 1913. Once again more new faces and much change in my life. The County School for Girls was a very elite establishment and the majority of pupils were fee-paying. Poor me; I was labelled one of those scholarship children. Such class consciousness was unbelievable even in those post Edwardian days.

It was, however, a most excellent school but oh such restrictions existed and it was more like living in Victorian days. My first encounter with the Headmistress made me feel such a worm – she was a very daunting person. The day I tried the scholarship she asked me a question which I answered with "Yes Miss" as I had always done with my previous teachers. She corrected me harshly by saying "You always say 'Yes Miss Mason'." Never having seen her before, how was I to know her name? The day before school opened for the Christmas term, I had to undergo the 'Head Mistress' exam. This was to determine which form I was to be placed in – it turned out to be the second form, the first was called the Remove. This was a very new world to me. From now on I mixed with the daughters of professional people like doctors, lawyers, ministers, architects and professors, also owners of wealthy trade establishments. Poor me!! If I had been surprised at some of the changes which I had experienced previously, I was now amazed – it was beyond anything that I had even dreamed or read about – it was an entirely new world.

Academically it did not daunt me; my education up to that point had been a thoroughly good one.

Here, however, were subjects such as geometry, algebra, Latin and changing teachers for each subject was a great novelty. I did not do French, I would have liked it but my father stated he wished me to do Welsh as a foreign language. What a farce, it was my mother tongue! All the same it soon dawned upon me that there was more to Welsh than just being able to read it and speak in our local dialect – much, much more. What I hated most of all was during English reading lessons, which the Head conducted herself; she constantly corrected my pronunciation of certain English words. She called it 'ironing out these provincialisms' from which remark I made up my mind that she was anti-Welsh; it made my blood boil.

As the free place lasted only three years, I had to satisfy the powers that be that my marks were good enough to be recommended for another year and so on. My stay there lasted six years, no thanks to anything except that I loved learning and not the Head. Most of the other Mistresses, as they were called, were not bad at all. I think that they all quaked before the Head. Now my pet hate was unfairness and I was the victim of this in my first term.

My form mistress was a German, Miss Zimmerman. When war broke out in 1914, she became naturalised and then called Miss Carpenter.

There were three 'Nellies' in school. Roberts, Griffith and me Nellie Rowlands. Nellie Griffith talked incessantly and sat right under the teacher's nose. All day long the teacher said "Nellie Rowlands stop talking". I never thought of correcting her, poor mutt that I was. When my report came home it said that my work was good but that I had to learn to be quiet. In a household such as ours, this meant that I didn't dare to try to justify myself. No-one would have believed me so I kept mum but I did wonder what remarks had been written on Nellie Griffith's report! This sense of injustice has stayed with me all my life. I just wish my Dad could read this. There was so much respect for parents then that I could never mention how I felt and thus clear the slate as it were. My father, I am sure, was quite proud of me in private but he was also my greatest critic.

My mother had older parents and she was the youngest of thirteen or fourteen children. She only knew four of them as the rest had either died very young or in early adulthood.

Her oldest surviving sister was in service with real gentry and she was a very aristocratic lady, beautiful and generally very much in command of things. She was forty-eight when she married an elderly widower who had a very successful business, drapery and shoes. At that time Anglesey where they lived was mainly agricultural and the shop supplied the many maids and farm hands with all they needed.

The money was safe as the people were simple and honest. They received their pay twice a year; the business flourished. We just called him Uncle as we found his name Ebenezer a source of amusement. He was so religious that he was a pain in the neck. We had been brought up strictly with a lot of religion but he was beyond everything we knew. He thought football was sinful and refused to give the village boys one penny towards a new ball. Sunday papers were 'of the Devil'. When the Chip Shop arrived it was in the same category as the pub. The fact that as a young man he had worked in Manchester had not broadened his mind. In spite of this he was very kind to poor people in the village whenever there was sickness and there was plenty of both, especially TB. Smiling on Sunday was taboo and having a holiday with them every summer was pure purgatory.

My maternal grandparents lived into their nineties. I don't remember my grandfather working; he was already old when I first knew him. He was a patrician-looking person. He had been a forester earning at most eighteen shillings a week. His employer, another of the landed gentry, owned a quarry and an enormous amount of land. Lloyd George introduced his budget giving five shillings to people over the age of seventy. My grandparents were well over this age. Because of this my grandfather's pension was cut by his former employer by five shillings, the measly two shillings coming in a cheque every thirteen weeks.

My writing illustrates the life of ordinary people at the turn of the century. Although both sets of grandparents had different environments, these two streams have been directed by genes into me and my generation and I am always conscious of being indebted to my forbears for whatever little that I may have achieved and I fear it is less than it should be.

My script is not in any chronological order but I just write what images my mind portrays.

So far it has reached the outbreak of the First World War when everything was turned upside down; the old order of things certainly passed away. New values came to bear upon everything and no family was quite the same afterwards. The world and its people appeared in a new dimension to us; the days of the British Empire were numbered but very few were aware of it at this time. News of happenings in faraway places came faster than before; soon there was wireless as it was first called; later 'telly' and videos and satellite. All mixed blessings.

There was a lot of poverty around us but it was often well hidden; there was also much drinking, mostly during Saturday. Many women drank but did not frequent the pubs; their daughters when they reached fourteen carried the beer in jugs through the streets openly for their mothers. These women hardly left their homes sunk into utter despair I suppose. Quite often they had hard working men for husbands, not always themselves drinkers. One in two of them were prominent members in the Chapels, taking part in services.

Mostly their children did not seem to suffer and grew up just like the rest of us. Looking back on upon this period makes me think that we belonged to the <u>ultra-respectable</u> – this did not prevent each class communicating freely with the rest of the natives; it was a very free little world in one sense.

Because my sister and I did not change schools when we moved to Hirael we did not make many friends of our age group, only those who attended Sunday school and had known when we lived in town. My younger sister and brother did attend the local school and grew up knowing far more local children than we did.

In spite of all its drawbacks this was not a miserable place to live in – I remember it more than tolerable in fact it was such a close gathering of humanity that it could be called Happy.

Nell – Ellen Grace Williams nee Rowlands was in her 97th year when she died. She was to write more but sadly broke her arm and never came out of hospital.

The next few accounts are about my Mum and Dad. Obviously I met them in 1940 when I was born but I said goodbye and thank you to my Mum in 1995 and to my Dad in 1997. These two people were the most loving, kind, generous and self-effacing people. They became firm friends with Nell from 1984 when our family circle grew to include Nell's son and Grandson.

DAD

It was Dad's eighty-fifth birthday and his wish was to visit his old school. He was six when the First World War started and lived at a time when there was a great deal of poverty. He told us it was called the 'Great War', nothing great about a war. He spoke of the Hoky Poky man (ice cream I think); of hoops and tops and a type of soup kitchen to which he was sent with a jug to get the only meal of the day. He remembered his father playing a one-day game of football for Gillingham, enabling him to earn a little money for the family to have a good Christmas, nothing compared to the acquisitive indulgence of the present day. He also sadly remembered times when his father being 'in drink' returned home ranting and raving and possibly beating his mother. The memories caused my Dad to be almost teetotal although his grandchildren will swear that two Sherries at Christmas lunch always guaranteed Granddad would lift his trouser legs, climb up on the table and dance. I can remember his liking for Mackeson stout if he was 'under the weather' and Wincarnis if he had been ill. His own father was a soldier and caught pneumonia whilst sleeping under canvas in the bad weather. It was said he had a full military Royal Engineers' funeral complete with gun carriage.

Dad was a loving and sensitive man; he cried a lot and had lots of sad memories he couldn't always share. He told me of the day he started school at 5 years old, going off with a roll and an apple and being sent home again as there wasn't a place for him until the following week.

His father kept chickens then and they were always being stolen or eaten by foxes. Once when he was ill, his father slept with him for comfort. In the middle of the night he was awakened by Grandpa whispering "Don't move, stay still". Suddenly his father jumped to the bottom of the bed screaming and shouting and attacking what he thought was a burglar with shining eyes. It transpired the burglar was his trousers with the moon shining on the buttons of his fly! Had he been drinking?

After his father died and Grandma was widowed with four children, Dad was sent to boarding school. He believed later that Gran had a boyfriend. Initially he did not realise he was to stay at school but when asked if he would like to join the band, he jumped at the chance. This meant, however, that he would be a boarder.

He did not realise the significance of this until a few days later. He became a Boy Soldier in the Duke of York's school – Hutton, the school moving temporarily from Dover because of the constant shelling. Every night he secretly visited the cloakroom at the end of a long corridor where he remained unseen and spent hours crying for his mother. He would close his eyes and pray that when they opened he would once again be at home. He was eight years old.

When predisposed to obesity, you must avoid breathing in the vicinity of a baker's shop. Even the slightest whiff of a doughnut can add two pounds in an instant! Dad had a passion for baker's shops. Everywhere we went he had to stop at the baker. Devon scones, Lardy Cakes from the West Country, Chelsea Buns from everywhere but Chelsea; Eccles cakes from goodness knows where, definitely not Eccles, and Frangipanes. Later is life he became a chauffeur, travelling throughout the UK. Everyone got parcels of Banbury Cakes by Special Delivery. Why such an obsession? On the birthday visit to Dover he showed us the baker's shop at the bottom of the hill. It emerged that when he was at school there he was just a crust away from starvation. He would often stand outside the shop looking in the window and praying someone would ask if he were hungry and buy him a bun. No-one ever did. Dad still had a deep-seated feeling of being abandoned. His whole family loved and adored him. When Mum died, this feeling returned never to go away.

We can find no records of Granddad playing football for Gillingham; maybe this and other memories were mixed up in the pain and agony of separation.

CHICKEN POX

Chicken Pox is an ugly and horrid sickness. Dad told me that out of one hundred and three boys he was the only one to catch the dreaded spots. Each day he was taken to the school hospital and the scales scrubbed with a hard brush causing a great deal of pain. This lasted for three weeks when he was left alone in the hospital ward.

RAINY DAY

"I remember a hay cart, us in our only (best) coats and boots Dad had cleaned, buttoned way above the ankle."

Mum recounted her journey to the graveyard in 1917 when she was eight, with older siblings and baby brother, a journey which was to leave her beautiful mother in a dark black hole, filled in by sombre-looking grave diggers and topped by a few flowers Dad had cut that morning.

No-one talked of grief, no-one asked Mum how she felt. She said Granddad always looked so sad. She cried for hours in the privy at the bottom of the garden; that was when she went on her own. The lavatory had two seats, side by side; one for the adults and a smaller one for the children. (In later years she was to take her little brother and then she sat on the adult's side.) This was 1917 and they were destitute. The older ones collected army greatcoats in a wheelbarrow and the whole family spent hours sewing on brass buttons until their fingers were raw. She couldn't remember when this ended but remembered the first Christmas without her mother when there was not even an orange between them and definitely no toys.

Her father was distraught and distracted. By the following Christmas a housekeeper was ensconced in the family home; slowly becoming a mother to the baby and anathema to her. Later the housekeeper turned step-mother compounded the mutual antipathy by frequently locking her in a cupboard or beating the backs of her legs with a strap.

The strap caused varicose veins; poverty instilled the value of thrift. In later years when another war came, she had children of her own. She was always cutting coupons from newspapers and magazines, every week collecting her divvy from the Co-op. Every scrap of paper was saved, every old stocking used to tie plants and even hold together the door number that had fallen apart where the screws had rusted.

Today was Mum's funeral, they opened an envelope marked 'Rainy Day – Save'.

A pound note sent from a tea manufacturer in return for dozens of tokens cut from tea packets.

Rainy day had come and gone, so had Mum. Sadly the currency was no longer in circulation.

BELOW STAIRS

Mum left home at just fourteen and went into service. She had to rise each day at four-thirty to make butter in a freezing larder. She scrubbed, polished and cleaned, each day having to whiten steps blackened by footsteps the previous day. Eventually she became a cook but remained in service until she was twenty-nine, when she left and went 'into service' for my Dad. She worked in Kent and London for models and film stars. Among the guests for whom she cooked were Noel Coward and Hardy Amies. She worked six and a half days each week and on her half day off she had to be in by ten o'clock. Her last employer, Barbara Blair wanted her to go to work in Miami but she chose to stay with my Dad, I am glad to say. She was a servant in the truest sense; everything she did in the most admirable and noble way, but she also 'knew her place'.

ROCHESTER BRIDGE

In the summer of 1995 we took my Dad on a trip to Rochester where we used to live. He remembered being at the opening ceremony in 1912 when he was four. The Bridge was opened by Prince of Wales (later George V).

ANNIE REMEMBERS

At the Drapers, the cost of my purchase was one farthing short of two shillings. I was given my change in pins and tape. I could have got one ounce of sweets for that!

I remember bread being weighed out in pieces to make up a Baker's Dozen (13).

1920-1940

Muriel came into our lives in 1969 when I moved to Morden with my first husband and my son. My second son was born in 1971 when Muriel and her friend Edith (neither of whom had children of their own) became surrogate Grandmothers to my children. Edith died in 1985; Muriel moved back to her home town near Gateshead and we have regular written contact.

MEMORIES FROM MURIEL

Muriel, now in her eighties, remembers going to her grandparents for Christmas and summer holidays. Muriel continues. They lived in Ipswich so it was an exciting journey on steam trains from Newcastle. My Mother's parents met us at the station and took us to their old rambly house and I had the attic room which had a lift up latch door from the landing and up a corkscrew stairway. There was also a very creepy cellar down lots of stairs and under the house. The house smelt of roses as they had a long back garden full of them; they seemed to be very strong scented in those days. My other grandparents lived at the other end of the town.

Their garden was the main attraction; they had ducks and a pool to paddle in, an apple tree and lots of fruit bushes. There were many Aunts and Uncles in the area and we all got together at Christmas. But most of all I remember the steam trains.

Doreen was part of the audience at a Women's group where I was giving a talk on a book I had published. She sent me an account to include in this book

DOREEN DELIGHTS US

When I was six years old my mother took me on a short holiday to Leigh on Sea in Essex. One day we went to a concert given by the Nigger Minstrels (you were allowed to use that word in those days). During the performance the children in the audience were invited onto the stage to do their 'party piece'. When it came to my turn, one of the minstrels asked me what I would like to do to which I replied "All things bright and beautiful". "Oh we don't know that one" he said. So I sang it unaccompanied and it was well received. Doreen is now in her eighties.

Mary was a friend of my second husband. With no children of her own she became a surrogate Grandma to my step-son and many other children in her local area of Downham, where I met her. She was a typical Londoner with a heart of gold and provided many wonderful memories for all the children who were lucky enough to be in her care. She died in the mid-nineties.

MARY'S MEMORIES

These are memories of a wonderful lady remembering her London childhood. She's gone now but her memory lives on in these words.

Small houses, lots of children, friendly neighbours always willing to help. I liked the old King and was sorry when he died. The police were always friends, always helpful and would clip our ear if we were found doing wrong. Lots of friends from the street and school; great times playing in the street. I never knew anyone from other parts of the world, or what went on in other countries.

Mums were great; Dad was boss and always had a newspaper which no-one was to touch until he had read it.

We had no money so there were no holidays but some school outings and we were often hungry. I got used to going without. There was no heating and we slept three to a bed to keep warm. No-one ever moved house until they married. We were all scared of the teachers and treated them with great respect.

I remember when I was three years old my Dad came home from the War (1st World War). I don't remember anything about this War but I went through the 2nd World War, which was dreadful and I would not want to do that again.

Winters were freezing but summers were very hot with lots of thunderstorms. I remember my brother made a radio with cat's whiskers and earphones; my Mum loved it. My pocket money was 1d (old penny) per week and I had to clean shoes and help with the housework for this. We only had sweets at Christmas; my penny pocket money had to be saved.

I did not have a boyfriend until I was 19 and although I could bring him home, I had to be in by 9.30 pm.

There was no 'permissive society'; there was a dreadful fear of being pregnant and thrown out of home and this was the best birth control. There was no talk of Gay people, Women's Lib or promiscuity.

We had very few photographs as no-one could afford a camera. Mum was very strict but loving and I had to go to Sunday school every week. The attitude to women was that they were slaves to the men folk.

Mary said that although they were poor and hungry, she was always very happy growing up.

When I met Nell in Benllech in 1984, I also met Alice. Alice, a typical Lancashire woman, says exactly what she thinks; a great friend of Nell, both being outsiders in a small community. Nell an outsider who, although Welsh through and through, had been born on the other side of the Straits. Alice a Lancastrian formed a bond with Nell to survive. Alice lived in Benllech and as will be seen from her script still has deep childhood wounds which may never heal. Alice reached 90 years in 2008 and died in July 2012.

ALICE'S WORDS

I lived in Lancashire in a house that belonged to the Coal Board. We had to go a long way to school, no buses in them days. My Dad was very funny about us being out after 9 o'clock. We hadn't much money as there was seven children. My Dad was awful to my Mum, used to hit her a lot. She couldn't go out at all and took in washing for a few shillings. I remember when I was little he left her in a ditch and my brother had to keep rubbing her to bring her round. He was a real bully. My Mum died at fifty-two and the Doctor told us not to wish for her back as she had suffered so much I was glad when I was old enough to leave home. Oh I can't write any more it hurts.

Laura was the niece of Nell's husband. I never met her but we talked often on the telephone after my husband had died. I have lost touch with her and sadly feel she has now died.

LAURA FROM MENAI STRAITS

Laura relates that she was born in 1924 at a small farm called Cae Gwydryn (field drinking glass) in the parish of Llan Ddeinolen (Church of the Saint) near Caernarfon in North Wales. She goes on to say – Welsh was my first language until I was about ten years old when I was taught English as a foreign language. As a small baby I moved with my family to a family farm. There was little time to play as we all helped on the farm. The little lambs were bottle fed and we treated them as 'our babies'. Little chickens were 'patients at the dentist'. In the Spring we helped in the fields by putting potatoes, carrots and other vegetables in the ground at the same time as looking for hidden treasure, which could have been a piece of broken cup. We also had to collect all the stones from the hay field, so that when it was cut the teeth on the machine would not be damaged. At summer time we had to help with the hay harvest. After father had cut the grass we all had to turn it over to dry before collection.

The vegetables too had to be harvested but we still sought out the treasure! Then came the corn harvest and it was great fun playing hide and seek in the stacks which were built like wigwams and we could go inside; any free time we had was spent going to Chapel, three times on Sunday. Prior to Sunday school we had The Band of Hope where we learned Tonic Sofa, to sing and read music. We also had to learn large pieces from the Bible to be recited in public after the evening service. This has encouraged me to continue and behave as a Christian all my life.

There were other meetings in both school and village. The Eisteddfod was a competitive gathering where we tried different fields of singing, recitation, music composition and poetry. In some of the larger gatherings there was needlework and woodwork. Two of the best known are Urdd Gobaith Cymry (the League of Youth), where points were awarded by county and the National Eisteffod where money is won. Both were held annually in North or South Wales, and the area in which they were held was expected to raise money for support. The two movements still hold gatherings but I don't think they are as well supported as in my time 1930-40.

When we went to the Grammar school the boys played football and the girls had hockey in winter and in summer it was cricket and tennis. If you had no money you had no balls! I was not good at sport so chose to be in charge of the drinks on the field and in the Winning Room if there were eats.

Other games I remember were Hop Scotch, Skipping with a very long rope and everyone trying to jump in and out. We also played Vi Vi, a round can on elastic which was worked up and down. If you were clever you played it sideways and up!

Bette is my Mum, Annie's niece. I went with Dad once to see her husband in a variety show. This family tie is only bound by Christmas cards and the occasional phone call when someone is born or dies!

COUSIN BETTE

My first memory is starting school in 1932, the day after my 5th birthday. I trotted off on a three mile walk from the farm I lived on to the nearest village school. I wore a round black velvet hat and a navy blue coat, under which, wait for it, was a woollen jumper, a gym slip, a flannelette petticoat, a liberty bodice, a vest, a pair of fleecy navy blue knickers with a pocket on the right leg, a pair of long black woollen stockings and on my feet a pair of black slip-on shoes. The stockings were held up by buttons stitched to the tops and a piece of broad elastic with a slit at each end, which fastened over the buttons on the stockings at one end and a button affixed to the liberty bodice at the other. Oh how I hated those black stockings and still do to this day; never wearing black stockings unless it is absolutely necessary. In the Infants school we used a slate and chalk and we took a bit of a rag to clean the slate.

The only time paper was used was to make a Christmas card. I guess we didn't waste paper in those days.

Bette goes on – when my grandchildren were small I looked after them while my daughter worked in the local hospital. One of the girls asked if she could watch 'Little Mouse and the Fairy' and was quite irate when I couldn't find it and I had to deal with a tetchy granddaughter all afternoon. Later that day I learned that the programme was 'Little House on the Prairie'.

I was in the middle of making a pantomime costume for my husband who usually played the Dame. My granddaughter asked what I was doing and I said I was making a skirt for grandpa. Later she said her mum would not let her have a pair of jeans. Trying to be diplomatic I said 'little girls don't wear trousers'. Her reply - "Grandpas don't wear skirts either"!

I visited London with my two children and my husband. An old aunt arrived at the house at which we were staying and she was shocked to see me grown up with children as she had still been sending me a 2/6d postal order at Christmas for years since I was a child!

Gwyn, my second husband and Nell's youngest son, died on 7th November 2001.

NO-ONE TOLD ME

I fell in love with a man who had the heart of a child. When we met his heart was frozen to contain a break caused when seven years old. His father was taken to hospital in 1936 when this man was five; his father had TB and was isolated from his family and friends. He never saw his Dad again. This child chased cats at the farm, walked on the top of hedges covered by drifting snow and peed in the same virgin snow making patterns with the hot steamy liquid. This was Snowdonia; lots of snow. After some time, when asking when Dad was coming home, all he got was "He is ill"; no more explanation. The child spent more time outdoors, more time alone. When he was seven, Dad died. Mam was left with three young sons. She could cope by putting away the only few photos she had, not talking about it again and trying to keep home and find a job. There was no pension. She returned to teaching being paid half the salary of male teachers because she was Mrs. No-one answered his questions; his broken heart was not salved; no assuaging his grief. His heart froze.

In middle age he received counselling for his grief but the memories of his father were buried so deep they never returned. His only recollection was of slicing off the tops of his Dad's prize tulips and a resultant 'thick ear'. He was unsure, however, if he had remembered this or been told by his Mam.

1940s

Maureen and I met at a spiritual event in 1980. She is a true friend and has always supported me. She is somewhat frail now having been through heart by-pass surgery but the spirit is still strong and she is still a great comfort to all her friends.

Maureen died in 2012 but not before she found some photos which were given to me by her daughter after the funeral.

THOMAS & IDA HEWETT AND THEIR DAUGHTER MAUREEN (WITH A TOUCH OF WORLD WAR TWO)

We lived in a small village south of London. The local mile stone at the side of the road in Lower Kingswood, Surrey said 'eighteen miles to Charing Cross'. This along with other direction posts disappeared overnight. Nobody saw them go; it was simply that war was coming. My Father volunteered for the RAF when I was five but he was turned down because he had flat feet. He volunteered as he knew he would not be 'called up' by the Government as he was in a reserved occupation maintaining ambulances for Netherne Hospital.

Until that time our life was happy with sunny summers and cold winters. Once a week we caught a green double Decker bus to market in the centre of Redhill. Mum also shopped in the village Co-op and collected her accumulated 'divvy' from the co-op in town, this money used to pay for a Marcel wave. I found this process fascinating, strands of her hair rolled into rollers and then a huge clips hanging on black cables from a large machine were clamped all over her head. The machine was then switched on and the hair 'cooked'! To me it looked like an instrument of torture. Prior to this, women had their hair crimped between two steel tongues heated on a gas ring appliance. The smell of singed hair was quite common.

This hairdressing horror I accepted but found it hard to cope with the small brown cardboard box which we had to carry at all times. Everyone said we were bound to be gassed but I did not know what they meant except that the box contained a horrible rubber thing with a celluloid-covered opening so we could see. There were straps which went round our heads to hold this gas mask in place and a metal round holder level with the mouth. They were awful. One day a unit arrived at our village, parked in the recreation ground.

The villagers were sent through it wearing their gas masks. It was quite frightening; it was a gas chamber.

Throughout all my war time childhood, my Mother was at my side. Like most upper working class wives when she had a child she chose to retire from work. (Note the definite class structure of that time.) She had been a sales manager of a team of girls, introducing Vim and a Fruit Loaf to the market. Missing the extra income, she persuaded my Father to take a lodger. At first he was shocked but agreed when she pointed out how much more could be done to the house they had built. This discussion followed by the arrival of a tall, fair, eighteen year old Dutch man; a banker's son who came to perfect his English. Mr Fontain was a lovely, well-educated man whom events overtook when Hitler's army invaded Holland; he was cut off from his family with no money. My Mother instantly agreed for him to stay, free of charge, until he could find work. We then found a local 'Bobby' on the door step who wanted to search his room as he was now classed as an alien. The policeman was distressed at this task as they played golf together. "Please don't tell Mr Fontain" he begged my Mother "he would be so upset".

Mr Fontain found help in London and when Britain declared war on Germany he decided to join up, enlisting in the Dutch Free Navy. He kept in touch and came to see us whilst on leave, my Mother spoiling him with his favourite 'Rabbit Welsh' as he called it. I loved him as he made a fuss of me, giving me his saved sweet ration. He never walked through our garden gate but always vaulted over it. The last time we heard from him was in nineteen forty when he was full of joy; he had met a Dutch nurse and they were to be married. He would bring her down next time but we never heard from him again. We presume he had been killed; this was war!

One week we got off our bus in Reigate looking for a dentist. As we stood by the closed railway crossing, a train passed travelling west and packed with soldiers. They had bandages on their heads and hands. I looked up into their faces and our eyes met. They looked so tired and in despair. (That vision haunts me to this day it was so vivid.) War indeed. My Mother made for the nearest Church to pray and light a candle for them and us. What we had seen was our men returning to Aldershot army camp after they were rescued from the beaches of Dunkirk.

We had no idea of this at the time; everywhere there were posters which said "Hush keep it dark, gossip costs lives"! It was later on Radio news. The situation was a great shock that the adults never explained to me. They then considered sending me away from home, evacuation it was called. How I persuaded my Mother to give up this idea I don't know but I never went.

The local authority introduced Air Raid Sirens; these went off quite frequently, sometimes false alarms but everyone was so jumpy; we were really waiting for invasion. At such times the light traffic would be taken off the main road (A217) into side roads, parking to allow emergency services through. My Mother, who was originally from Birmingham, went out to these cars with trays of tea offering words of comfort to allay people's fears. They appreciated it; she enjoyed it too and I liked helping when I came home from school.

At night the German bombers droned into our consciousness. We didn't make for the shelters but lay with blackout curtains open (lights out of course). I watched from my bedroom window. We were on a North Downs hill and saw the bombing of London Docks.

What a different firework display, night after night; we tried not to be afraid. Dad was a voluntary fireman at the hospital and took turns as an Air Raid Warden and when he was not there Mum and I clung to each other.

One afternoon my Mother's 'tea' found a Jewish family, husband, wife and mother, full of fear and whose house had been badly bombed. My Mother offered our home as a place to have a rest; they were delighted. I moved into the little bedroom, dividing the house in two.

We had an Air raid shelter at the end of the garden and my father threw the dugout spoil over the top as instructed on the leaflet provided. All the children thought this was marvellous, standing on this artificial mound waving to the RAF Spitfires coming quite low over us and the allotments of the Working Men's club behind us and chasing the German fighters. We had no sense of danger as the pilot fired bullets at his target. No sirens had sounded, "This is fun; this is more like it" we said jumping and shouting words of encouragement. We then scattered into the shelter as another German fighter shot up the roofs of our homes and the siren sounded. We later discovered that the Battle of Britain was on in earnest.

Every day we watched the planes weaving and diving, quite fascinated by it all as we walked to and from school. The boys' future now moved from driving trains to pilots and the girls wanting to be Wrens in the Royal Navy; we liked water and the uniforms were so smart! Our gang – June and Maureen Clarke whose father was in the Navy; John Tregarther whose father was in the RAF, and me: and we did all the things country children do. Across the main road was a foot path alongside an overgrown meadow, destined to be a building site. A stack of window frames covered with a tarpaulin which although tied down, gave entry to small children and became a climbing-frame-come ship. Nobody suspected and it was better than climbing trees and so secret. We kept stores of scrumped apples and biscuits in a tin box and bottles of pop. Sheer bliss to us kids.

Our lodgers, the Strawsons, insisted we all went to the Air Raid shelter when the siren sounded. Mr Strawson was terrified of spiders, as was my Mother and of course, me. The shelter had bunk beds down both sides and I slept on an old wooden ironing board placed across the bottom end.

One night the adults were having a heated political debate when suddenly my Mother took her rolled up newspaper and began hitting Mr Strawson around the head and shoulders. Mr Strawson thought she had gone mad and after being restrained she apologised explaining that there was the biggest spider she had ever seen crawling on him.

Although the air raid was in full swing, Mr Strawson, nothing less than six feet tall, flew out of the entrance and proceeded to shake his heavy overcoat over the vegetables with money flying in all directions. We children had fun looking for it the next day. From then on every nook and cranny in the Anderson was stuffed with cotton wool and incense cones burnt every day. We were amazed but there were no more spiders! Not long after this the Strawsons found a new family house below Reigate hill to which we were invited for tea and inspection. I was in awe of the pitch roofed artist's studio built over the garage. By now I was showing artistic talent, inherited from my Mother, and I dreamed about that building for a long time. I did become an artist many years later.

Our next lodgers, sent to us by villagers, were Mr & Mrs Ricardo from Holland. Nearby in Smithy Lane was a large property bought by the Dutch Shipping Offices. Little did we suspect it was a cover for MI6, visited often by strangers and where worked our lodgers. They were very nice and offered to teach me Dutch which I declined (foolish me). He worked as an Air Raid warden and we did not suspect they were part of Intelligence until the offices closed.

Other interesting visitors to the house: Mr Brewer whose father had been a prison governor in India during the Raj. Their lives had been threatened many times and he insisted on all landing lights being left on and looked under all the beds each night. Although he was harmless, my Mother was glad to see him go. Another fellow was very jolly, Captain Dutrick another Dutch man. He told us many tales but was arrested on returning to Holland after the war; he had been a double agent, his wife was German and her family, still in Germany, had been blackmailed. At this time we heard that Mr Ricardo had waited in Holland until the Hun had overrun the country and taken the last freighter out of Rotterdam. He had been an official with Shell Oil Refineries. The Ricardos stayed with us for three years when they got a house in Chipstead Lane.

Sadly Mr Ricardo died on his return to Holland but we later visited his wife in Doorn. When they left my Mother decided against any more lodgers and took a stall at the Saturday Epsom Street market. She sold hand-painted fancy goods and with an electric hand-held engraver carried out her beautiful copper-plate handwriting; she was in great demand as fancy goods were not manufactured anywhere because all factories had been turned over to munitions.

At one time a returning German bomber off-loaded bombs on the village. It was a dramatic night with incendiaries falling on the village hall, barns and hayricks. This was followed by two oil bombs which fell at the back of two bungalows, splashing the walls but not exploding. The next huge bomb landed in the allotments near the Dutch Shipping Offices and our 'ship'. It stuck upright in the soft earth and protruded some eight feet. Half the village was evacuated whilst the Bomb Disposal boys did their stuff. We prayed they would be successful so our homes would not be damaged. The Village hall was packed and thank God no-one was killed.

Our next family adventure was a trip to Aunt Lilly, Uncle George and Cousin Yvette in the Isle of Man where there was an internment camp for Italians. We were at War with Italy as their leader Mussolini was a fascist who had visited Hitler in the thirties and made a pact with the Nazis. Some people in our area heard we were going and asked my Mum to take a food parcel to their family, to which my Mum agreed. We packed a sea-faring trunk taken from the loft and all my clothes were laid out with tissue paper between. The trunk had two built-in padlocks and was tied around with string and labelled.

A friend took us to Paddington from where we had to travel by night, because of the blackout. We travelled via Crewe to Fleetwood, not Liverpool as normal; changing trains in the pitch dark. Mum and Dad tipped the porter to ensure our luggage travelled with us. The train was packed to suffocation; service men were sitting on luggage in the corridors.

The tipped porter found us a dining car and Mum made me a bed on the table but it was impossible to sleep. A drunken Merchant seaman was singing and ranting about his experiences.

After a while my Mum took a flannel and towel out of our hand luggage, had a chat with him about sobering up because of me; he took the offer. He was covered in oil as he had been torpedoed twice. He said he was from Glasgow and although he had two leather suit cases, we doubted they were his originally but spoils of war. He had everything in them; nylons, yards of silk cloth, perfume etc. some of which he wanted to give my Mother for her kindness. She refused fearing the black market might be involved. He was now sober and whilst I slept he chatted to my parents for most of the night.

The next day we had to queue dockside in Fleetwood for four hours whilst the troops boarded the ship first. The remainder took a chance on whether or not we got a place. Good old Uncle knew the Chief Engineer, however, and had asked him to allow us to use his cabin which he did, thank the Lord. My father was always sick on sea crossings and he could get his head down. It was a terrible journey, ships having no stabilisers then. A storm hit as soon as we left harbour with a full load of cargo and passengers. There was also the risk of enemy mines off the major port of Liverpool.

The Irish Sea is purported to be one of the worst crossings in the world but the crew took charge of me and I had a lovely time seeing the huge engines working and walking on the tossing decks with huge strong hands holding me. I loved the salt sea whipped up into my face and squealed with delight. Our relations saw the ship on the horizon but it took five hours before we docked in Douglas harbour. When we arrived, receiving hugs from our loved ones who offered up prayers for our deliverance, we had another shock.

Next morning my Mum went to unpack our trunk and saw immediately all the clothes at the top had gone. Clothing too was rationed; she sat down and wept. My Auntie took charge, giving her a cup of tea, and then phoning all their friends on the Island (my Uncle was a Manxman). In no time at all I had a complete new set of clothing, it was marvellous. Nobody could work out how they had unlocked it, my Dad saying to a practised thief it would be easy. We enjoyed that holiday very much but it would be ten years before we returned to the Island, my Dad then in the beginnings of Parkinson's disease.

The area in which we lived suffered terribly because of flying bombs or Doodle Bugs as we named them. These were brought down by anti-aircraft fire, from a station below Reigate Hill.

At this time, I was unable to persuade my Mother and was sent to stay with Uncle Tom's family at Northfield, Birmingham but that's another story.

My early days with my family, surrounded by love and sacrifice

PEANUTS

At six years old I played beside the river Medway together with a group of other kids and maybe my sister, but she was only three. We hung over the edge of a pontoon scooping peanuts from the river, the ancient name Merwge means deep water; deep water meant nothing to kids with no fear. Rochester had docks then and it was cheaper for boats to unload their cargo and transport it by train than for the boats to manoeuvre their way up to London. It still provides the cheapest and quickest port facility in the country. Peanuts, I can taste them now and although the husks were wet, they still crunched between our teeth, the dry powder exploding around our mouths. We spat out the casings and the silky coating could either be removed with the tongue and ejected in the same direction or, crunched together with the beautiful nut that came free, via the river, from goodness knows where.

"Mum says it is rude to spit." Mum doesn't know we spit; Mum doesn't know we are here, she thinks we are at Marie's. It was about three miles to the river from where we lived; we walked. Very few cars then, buses yes but not often. Besides, we didn't have any money. This was the forties. Sun Pier, it's still there. I am a grandma now but revisited recently. The pier is the same, newly painted though and bounded by an office supplies company and a radio station. I walked along the pier and down the wooden ramp to the pontoon. No peanuts, just dozens of swans looking for bread. Would they settle for dry roasted?

MUM

I close my eyes and I can see the place in which we lived when I was four. There was a coal fire with a fender around, complete with red leatherette-topped boxes at each end on which we sat in winter to keep warm. We had to change sides when either the left or right cheeks or arms became so red we could not bear it any longer. No-one moved away; although the room was small, the fire was not big enough to send heat very far. There were brass tools – a fork on which we toasted bread with a handle not long enough to prevent our hands burning. There was a brush to keep the hearth clean and a small shovel for the coke derivative of coal. Mum always polished the brasses and brushed the red mat covered in an assortment of small holes made when red hot embers jumped from the fire in an explosion of orange. We watched 'children going to school'; tiny bright sparks travelling up the chimney and disappearing into the darkness as the flames caught the soot.

Back to Mum. She had pneumonia; the Doctor came, she was sick. We were all very cold; the coke had all gone and there was no fire. Mum wrapped us in our outdoor coats and sat us in the corner.

"Look after your sister, I won't be long." I remember her face, she was such a beautiful woman but that day she cried and wheezed and coughed. She put on her old and only coat and a scarf around her head. She looked in her purse, climbed on the fender and took a tin box from the mantelpiece. She looked at us and cried some more and then pushed the blade of a knife into the slot, tipping the box at the same time. Money slid out and quickly into her purse and off she went. She was pushing the pram but without the baby. Where was she going? "Go to Nurse Young if you are upset, I will be quick." Nurse Young lived next door. I thought she was very old; sixty seems very old when you are four. Her house was dark; curtains closed most of the time. In later years I felt she had auditioned for the part of Miss Haversham.

I looked at my sister and started to sing Nursery Rhymes but then climbed up and put on the wireless. The time went so quickly. A noise at the door caused us to jump; a key in the lock, it was Mum. She juggled with the pram and brought it into the small hall. Mum was pale, almost white and still coughing. Many years later I learned that she had walked to the Gas Works to buy coke.

She had left us alone; she had no alternative; she was not well enough to push the pram and cope with two small children. Dad was in the army in Catterick. A brave woman, always with a bad cough but she was a '20 a day' girl. Woodbines, or did she roll her own then? Woodbines then came in packs of 5, wrapped in thin paper but never with health warnings.

VIOLETS

When I was six Dad said I could have pocket money; 6d was what I had, six old pennies; two hundred and forty pennies to the pound. Mum gave in to my pleas and eventually agreed that I could spend the money. I got the bus outside our house; the fare was 1/2d. I got off at Star Hill and walked to the shops. There was a flower lady on the corner and I bought a bunch of violets for Mum, costing 4d. My fare home was another 1/2d. What happened to the other 1d? I really can't remember. Perhaps I saved it for another day. We did not have sweets then; everything was still 'on ration'. Everyone had a Ration Book and there was a weekly allowance for sugar, butter, tea, meat, sweets and clothes. People would swap or borrow coupons and were encouraged to grow their own vegetables; the diet sparse but healthy. In Rochester there was a weekly cattle and sheep market with other stalls. I can still 'feel' the celluloid doll I bought, it was about 50cms long, unclothed and with blue eyes that opened and shut. Perhaps it cost a penny?

ELECTRICITY

My Aunt died very young and left four
children. I have a vivid memory of being on
the floor beside her bed (or was it my little
sister?). I wore a Liberty Bodice, a funny
type of thick vest complete with rubber
buttons. I poked my finger into a socket and
can only remember everyone screaming and
feeling very shaky. "It was them buttons
what saved her" said another of the Aunts.

In 1999 I was awarded a Master's Degree in the Science of Education and Training. I met Shelagh at the awards ceremony at Guildford Cathedral.

FROM SHEELAGH CLARKE – A MEMORY OF MAY 1946 GROWING UP IN CHURCH ROAD BALLYBUNION, CO KERRY, EIRE

Come each month of May, along with the fine weather, my mother would announce the family's first visit of the year to the Shell Valley. This was a mile away from the village. The excitement was great as my four sisters and I helped my mother to get ready a picnic. The picnic lunch box consisted of sandwiches made of butter and jam. Mi-Wadi orange juice appropriately diluted with water, a flask of tea, home-made apple tart and scones, and finally, periwinkles. A bag with swimming togs, towels and rug was also packed. My father and only brother never accompanied us on this trip. It was purely a girls' outing. We all dressed in our summer frocks and sometime around 11 o'clock in the morning my mother and five sisters started out on the long walk to the Valley. As we trekked along the main street and came to Cissie Mac's Corner Shop; my mother entered the shop and bought home-made ice cream for all.

This was for us a delicious treat. As the tide was in we walked along the cliffs of the Old Golf Course. On arriving at the Shell Valley the rug was ceremoniously spread out on the ground. We all sat around my mother as the picnic began. On this occasion, as per usual, the Mi-Wadi and sandwiches were first devoured. The apple tart followed. After eating our fill my mother stretched out on the rug while the five of us girls raced each other to the top of the valley before sliding at breakneck speed back down over the sand. This we did over and over again until exhausted. I can still recall the feeling in my tummy of thrilling excitement. We then gathered shells of all sizes, shapes and colours. We then had finished off the eating with a feast of periwinkles which we picked out of their shells with tiny pins.

Later, as the evening drew near, we tidied up, packed our bags and began the first part of our journey home along the golden beach lapped by the mighty Atlantic. We stopped on our way for all six of us to splash and swim in the beautiful blue waters of the ocean. This refreshingly rounded off a glorious day in May. Back home later we fell into bed exhausted but happy.

As a footnote to my reminiscences when I recently returned to revisit the happy haunts of my girlhood, I discovered that our Shell Valley is no more. It has been swallowed up by the Golf Links as it extends its tentacles along the shore. Our happy valley is gone never to return – except in daydreams. (May 2004)

In 1963 aged 23, I was working in the office of a travel agency in London. I was introduced to a young Italian woman, dressed in dark green with a cheeky tartan beret. She had come to improve her English which I felt was far better than mine! She stayed for some time, we became good friends. Forty-nine years later the friendship is still as strong. She lives in Amalfi with her husband, her lovely children having moved to different parts of the world, one working at NASA in the US. We have exchanged visits; every year she sends me some lovely Italian sweets and a wonderful photo of her family. We don't speak often but we know we can always be there for each other if needed. This is her poignant contribution.

LINA

My beloved Dad was in the army, embarked on the S/S Alberto di Giussano, when I was due to be born. He came on a special leave but apparently I was not in a hurry, so the leave was over, he left and I was still in my mum's belly. He had brought some real good coffee which my mother had intention to save for my Christening but her intention faded in the morning when she made a nice cup of coffee thinking there was plenty. In the end the coffee finished and I wasn't born yet. At last the big day arrived; not the right one apparently, for my granny was busy with her stall at the local fair and she had to rush to my Mum's bed with the midwife. Mum was thin, very thin, and everybody thought it was a miracle when I opened my eyes. I weighed more than 8 pounds and in spite of the war and lack of good food, I grew healthy and fat! No news from my Dad! He knew I was born, he was also happy that my Mum had given me her mother-in-law's name.

In 1944 the Royal Family was in Ravello and Prince Umberto di Savoia visited my grandfather. My granny asked him about my Dad. He promised he would check the matter when in Rome. He kept his promise but what he wrote drove my Mum to desperation.

"No official news on the sailor Francesco Camera. He might be a prisoner or 'Missing!'"

With the Prince's word in her heart my Mum considered herself a widow but never lost the hope to see the husband again.
It was July 1945 when the husband of a friend of my mother told her that her husband had suddenly turned up. Then seeing tears on my mother's cheeks she added "don't worry, I am sure the Virgin Mary will hear your prayers, next week it's her feast day!"

My Mum thought it was impossible and on the feast day she put my elder brother and me to bed as usual. It was not yet midnight when somebody knocked at the door. My father's youngest sister called my Mum and with excited voice she asked us to wake up. A few minutes later my granny's old sister entered our house and soon after my grandfather. I remember I was in my aunt's arms and the old lady dragged my sleeping brother. We were wearing our pyjamas and my Mum put on her overall and off we went to grandfather's house.

I was nearly 4 and it all happened sixty years ago but I have a clear memory of every minute.

I also remember the pyjamas I was wearing; white and pink and I distinctly see the dolls on the pavement square which the street vendor hadn't put away after the feast! All the lights were on in my grandfather's house; his brothers, sisters and his Mum were around him and there he was…my beloved Dad whom I had only seen in pictures.

I still remember my disappointment; the man who wanted to embrace me was not my Dad, or at least was not the handsome black haired young man of the pictures. I had a skinny, bald old man in front of me. "That's not my Dad". I cried and ran into Mum's arms. She was unhappy too. She never forgave my Dad for the fact that he had gone to his parents' house first. Their love was strong though and for years after I heard her saying "You wanted to check if I had been faithful to you in the period you were a prisoner of the Serbs" and every time I heard my dearest Dad answer "You know I went there because I didn't want to shock you! The war had stolen my youth, my health and my beauty".

Gillian was another kind and spiritual friend, introduced by Maureen. She had many illnesses and found living in the London suburbs very difficult. She moved to the North Country with her husband Allan where she remained only a short time before she died in 2006 followed by her husband in 2008.

GILLIAN RECALLS

It was a red and white bus that brought my mother and me from London to Blewbury, an agricultural village lying at the foot of the Berkshire Downs, halfway between Oxford and Reading. Depositing us at a modern Esso Petrol Station, the bus journeyed onwards to Wantage and beyond, whilst my mother juggled with various favourite toys, packages and suitcases until we reached the house where Gran was waiting to welcome me into her home for however long it took. I was being evacuated.

Having recently come out of hospital after a stay of 16 weeks for Lymph gland trouble (Kaolin Poultices and bed rest being a preferable option to extensive throat surgery), I was not too happy at being separated from my mother yet again and made no bones about letting all and sundry know.

I little realised at the time how fortunate I was to be living with caring grandparents and in relative safety from bombs and things that go bump in the night, whilst my mother had to return to the drudgery of compulsory work in a Munitions factory and my father travelled around the country on war work involving National Security. Gran and Granddad must have seen great changes by moving from an old cramped tumbledown cottage with pump and loo outside, into their new home, a modern-built council house by the side of the main road. Even though these days we wouldn't call it much to write home about, there was a lot more space to bring up a family of two daughters and a son. At least Granddad didn't have to worry about knocking his head on low beams and the roof was pretty sound too.

I don't know whether the council forbad keeping animals but until she moved, Gran had always had dogs, each one in turn a black and white spaniel and each in turn called Joey. So now, if there was a restriction on pets, she got around it by keeping a succession of blue budgies, also called Joey, and a solitary goldfish – quite likely called Josephine.

These houses were probably some of the first council properties to be built since the end of the 1914/1918 war and living conditions still left a lot to be desired. Water still had to be pumped by hand, but at least the pump was now in the kitchen next to an indoor sink (no taps) and draining board. The kitchen also boasted a bathroom complete with bath – but again what use were taps? To get hot water it had to be pumped and then carried from the kitchen into the dining room, heating in a boiler built into a massive coal-fired range, surrounded by an equally massive brass safety guard. The shortage of hot water is probably the reason why my mother used to refer to her having a DP or duck's puddle with about six inches of water if you were lucky – enough hot water for a proper bath being saved for special occasions. The black-leaded remnant of a Victorian age also provided oven and hot plates for cooking fabulous tasting meals, bread and cakes and for heating Gran's shiny flat irons. Puts you in mind of a modern day Aga with attitude! Fuelling this old workhorse with coal made more economic sense (although more work) than using the expensive paraffin-fired stove, also installed in the kitchen since Granddad was now working for his brother-in-law delivering coal!

Another advantage had to be that instead of the loo being at the bottom of the garden it was now designated a specially designed water closet complete with two seats, built for convenience (no pun intended) outside the back door and kept regularly supplied with quarter pages torn from old gardening magazines (ouch?) and guess whose job it was to thread them by the corners with string? Jeyes Fluid was used by the gallon to keep everything hygienic. I suspect that it may have been this plus a huge compost heap that contributed to the wonderful flowers and vegetables Granddad grew in his fairy tale and productive garden. Chenile abounded everywhere, from table cloths, mantle shelf covers, antimacassars, curtains etc. In the front room stuffed birds and animals given as wedding presents, kept me silent company when I was banished there once for trying to pick some icing off my birthday cake, made and decorated by Gran. She may have had the misshapen hands (and feet) that come from many years of arthritis, but she sure knew how to wield an icing bag or send you packing when required.

Incidentally, despite her hands she had the most attractive and well-formed handwriting I have ever seen apart, of course, from the deliberately calligraphic art.

It was a short walk from Gran's house to Mrs Hawkins' Infants School in Blewbury village, next to St Michael's Church. My mother had already taught me how to read at an early age but sums were a different kettle of fish and something that bugged me all through school. I have made painful contact with more rulers and corners than I care to remember. Sometimes school could be put off a little longer by taking the narrow lane around by the watercress beds, watching the ducks swimming and up-ending for their breakfast and the bees from the nearest beehive, humming as they worked the wild flowers. At some time the brook had been made safe from adventurous children by thatching the walls with straw; quite a scratchy deterrent. The beds had to be closed down some years later when it was found that the water was not as pure as was necessary and had now become contaminated by a local pig farm.

Even in the summer, every morning before going to school Gran would give me Malt and Cod Liver Oil out of a large dark brown jar and every Friday there was a dose of Syrup of Figs and DP. The Malt and Cod Liver Oil certainly kept the cold out during the winter; unfortunately it had the effect of making me as fat as a mile, with spare tyres to match.

This was not calculated to endear me to my classmates; not only was I an outsider but I was fat as well – a prime candidate for bullying – so what changes? The crunch for me came when, for some reason I was chosen to play Little Miss Muffet in the Christmas play. Clothing was rationed as well as food, and extra coupons were hard to come by unless you were in the know. Even the inventiveness of my Grandmother was unable to make the far too small obligatory Liberty bodice and suspenders, plus the (tiny) borrowed costume, big enough for comfort. I spent the entire evening in agony wrestling with buttons, hooks and eyes that popped and tight elastic in tight knickers. I vowed never to play a starring role again! I much preferred the freedom of walking on my own through fields of sunshiny corn waving over my head and making friends with the animals grazing higher up on the Downs.

It was safe then for small people to ramble and play make-believe either with friends or on their own. A couple of times I was fortunate enough to meet my Gran's father, Great-granddad Gad Street, a shepherd looking after his flocks high up on the Downs. I don't suppose we talked much – he was a man of few words anyway, and I was greatly in awe of this kindly giant with masses of white hair, beard and sideburns. I don't really remember much of my Great-grandmother Charlotte Street who was an herbalist and wise to the ways of women. I like to think that my great interest and subsequent practice of herbal medicine may have come from her genes.

The white and red bus in due course returned my mother and me to the city and a totally different landscape. Normality now centred around finding somewhere habitable to live that was free of bed bugs inhabiting the wallpaper, or a place made safe from the bomb damage that surrounded us.

I went back for a brief summer holiday when I was about 12 years old but by then I was so full of my own ideas and resentful of the fact that I was not allowed to stay under canvas on the Downs in company with an archaeological dig, and so returned home again from a since forgotten way of life.

It has been a wonderful treasure to recover and I am glad to have had the opportunity to revisit this magical place of childhood.

UNCLE JACK

We stayed with Uncle Jack when we left
London to get away from the bombing. I was
tiny but we stayed a good few years. He
worked as a Railway Guard and when I was
a little older, he used to take me with him to
see the station and once let me blow his
whistle. The trains were very noisy, lots of
steam. Uncle Jack taught me a rhyme; I
have taught this to my children and
grandchildren. I have looked everywhere to
see if I could find this but perhaps he made
up the rhyme.

There was a little boy, 5 years old
He wore a little petticoat to keep him from
the cold
He went into the woods to build a little
church
And he asked all the dicky birds to help him
with the work
The hen was the parson, the cock was the
clerk
The monkey blew the candle out and left
them in the dark!

This sounds much better with a Lancashire
accent where 'clerk' rhymes with 'derk'!

1950s

These are some more childhood memories

SMELLS OF THE PAST

Tarmac? The hot black smelly stuff used for mending roads, pouring off the back of a tipper truck, steaming and sticky. As a kid this smell was accompanied by a loud rumbling noise as a huge steam roller moved back and forth flattening the tar mixed with small stones. I am not sure if these are still used but you can see them at Steam Fairs. My baby sister called them 'roller steamers'. We were not supposed to tread on it until it set. Of course we often did and Mum went mad if we got it on our shoes leaving tiny stones stuck to our already shabby carpet.

Coal? Mum and Dad had a coal cupboard. The coal man would come through the back gate and into the kitchen with huge hundredweight sacks on his shoulder and an empty sack on the top of his head, supposedly to stop him getting dirty! It didn't work. We watched him carry the load and counted the number for Mum as he shot a sack full into the cupboard. A really tiny house, very small kitchen and the coal cupboard was next to the larder. I was torn between sticking my head in the coal cupboard, inhaling what I thought was a captivating smell and standing in the larder which often smelled of warm jam tarts and sometimes boiled ham cooling down.

Freshly washed sheets? On the rare occasions that I collect my dry washing from the line in my garden, I bury my head deep into the sheeted memory of my long dead Mum and remember the love and safety of her clean washing. These beautiful white cotton bed covers were lovingly ironed as soon as they came off the line; starched if she had time. Often, if we were home when Mum 'made the bed', she would let us lie down and she would wave the top sheet up and down, completely covering us. This would cause cotton flutters above us and butterflies in our tummies. I carried on this tradition with small grandchildren and a duvet; I knew just what they meant when they said "My tummy tickles".

Soap Flakes? It was a luxury to have a bath alone. My sister and I shared a bath for a long time. For a special treat Mum or Dad would add some Lux Soap Flakes and whisk up a frenzy of bubbles with a copper stick. Sometimes we would have a bath each but it took such a long time to boil a copper full of water and it was costly.

Hot Wet Washing mixed with Jam Tarts?
Coming home on the bus from school, always upstairs often with the windows steamed on the inside and covered with raindrops on the outside, the air was thick with stale cigarette smoke. I anticipated my lovely warm house a few minutes from the bus stop. Running across the road, not much traffic then, hanging on to my satchel and beret, my blazer barring the precipitation from dampening my school blouse. Mum was always there when I rang the bell; in her overall, constant with a beautiful smile. My senses were greeted with a mixture of boiling washing, fresh cooked pastry and just a hint of Weights or Woodbines, stubbed out just as I rushed across the road.

FOOD GLORIOUS FOOD

Summers were long, we played tennis and cricket on the green outside our house; happy days. No children could have been loved more. Dad worked so hard; children don't realise the seriousness of life. Our kitchen was so small with a stone larder and one of my Dad's DIY efforts in the corner. No fridge but a 'safe' – a wooden box with two shelves and a wire window to keep out the flies. This was kept in the shade just outside the back door. I recall the smell of sour milk, bottles with cardboard tops, leftover meat crawling with maggots as some-one had left open the larder door! Sticky fly papers hung from the ceiling, dead flies staying longer than was healthy but postponing the day when new papers were added to the shopping list.

Mum cooked for England! She was a wonderful cook. Such a small space in which to create. Often at Christmas there were fifteen people at one sitting. Mum managed to feed us all turning the bathroom into an extended kitchen area. She put a board across the bath and used this as a serving table.

She made the best Yorkshire pudding this side of Edinburgh; her pastry was so light it floated from her oven together with jam tarts that floated into the mouths of all the children in our road. She made pies and cakes, peppermint lumps, fudge, toffee and toffee apples. Our welcome home from school accompanied a homely smell of cooking.

We ate for England! Oven busters (a rather large cut of beef) on Sunday with cold beef sandwiches for tea and cold roast potatoes refried for supper if the neighbours' kids hadn't eaten them cold. Cold meat, chips, pickle and tomatoes on Monday; Shepherd's Pie on Tuesday. I can't remember Wednesday and Thursday but she made a wonderful Steak and Kidney pie and we always had home-made fish and chips on Friday. We weren't Catholic but it was traditional.

I ate for England and Wales and got bigger and bigger! I can now see that it was necessary to 'bulk up' the meal with suet pastry and puddings to make up for the lack of meat. Strange that I am now vegetarian.

Those lovely long summers when we played in Rosehill Park for the whole day, climbing trees and making a camp with a picnic of bottled water and jam or sugar sandwiches.

CHRISTMAS

Wonderful times, pillowcases on the settee downstairs, always full on Christmas morning. Postal orders from Aunts and Uncles, 5/- (five shillings) 10/- (ten shillings) and sometimes £1. We always had an orange an apple and sweets at the bottom. As we grew older and we thought more sophisticated, we got a small box of Cadbury's Dairy Milk. My Godmother lived in Knightsbridge and shopped at Harvey Nicholls. One Christmas we had crackers from there with lovely jewellery inside. One year I lost a postal order and we had to go through all the scrunched up wrapping paper to find it before it went into the dustbin.

SEASIDE

The St Helier Estate, Morden was beautiful, so many trees and greenery. There were many happy children there in the forties and fifties. There were also so many poor families. Each year there was a free outing to the sea side, sometimes up to 40 coaches. All children on the estate were entitled to go. My Mum and Dad would not let us go. They said we were luckier than the other children as we always had holidays. I am sure she was right but I really did want to go.

PAST EIGHT O'CLOCK

My darling Mum suffered terribly with varicose veins and ulcers and I remember her beautiful legs were constantly bathed and bandaged. Dad did night work and one evening after he had gone to work and we were tucked up in bed I heard my Mum shouting. My little sister was fast asleep, so I ran downstairs. As I opened the door to our little front room I saw Mum sitting on the settee with her foot in a bowl and with blood pumping out to the rhythm of her heart, into the bowl and onto the carpet. I wanted to scream, I wanted to cry. I was ten years old. "Listen love" she said calmly, "put on your shoes and coat and run up to Doctor G's and tell her it is an emergency". It was cold and dark outside and I ran past the ten houses without looking left or right. I banged on the door and it seemed ages before anyone came. I implored the Doctor to come quickly to see my Mum, fearing that Mum would die whilst I was away. Doctor G stemmed the flow, dressed the wound and I watched in awe. "Your Mum will be fine now but Mrs F what on earth are you thinking letting a child of this age be up at this time of night!"

HOW EMBARRASSING

Mum won some money on the football pools. We had new suits with two skirts; they were grey and one skirt was straight with a small split at the back, the other was pleated. We also had a bike each. We lived on a council estate and no-one had much money. The bikes were such a novelty that all the kids came out to see us ride them along the cycle path. My younger sister was off and away down the path with all the kids running behind her trying to keep up. I was fat, accident prone and scared stiff. It was all I could do to stay upright. My sister was on her way back and I had only just got my feet on the pedals. I could not manage to turn the pedals the whole way and rode without turning them once; left foot down at the back, right foot down at the front. Fifty years on my sister still finds this embarrassing but at least she can now talk to me about it. I did redeem myself later when in my forties I started to ride again and often did forty miles on a Saturday afternoon; on my mountain bike the pedals went all the way round!

AT RISK

We had a tiny house but we were lucky to
have an inside lavatory and a bathroom.
The water was heated by a gas copper and
often Mum caught her arm on the side,
swearing under her breath. We got to learn
some of these words as we got older and
harder to control! I was being silly, as I still
do from time to time and dancing in the
water. My sister was laughing at me but this
turned to screams, mostly from me as I fell
and landed buttocks down right on the lid of
the copper. I can't remember the pain now
but never forgot the incident. I was off
school for a while as I could not sit for days,
and had to lie face down on the floor waiting
for the huge blister to heal.

SPOILED BRATS

Nearly every Sunday morning my sister and I had breakfast in bed. Although now a vegetarian I can still remember the taste of the well-cooked link sausages dipped in runny egg and buying them at Ralph's which later became one of the first Tesco's. Dad also cleaned our shoes. He was a military man and always had highly polished shoes, still shining brightly when he was almost blind. In the rush and tear of a working Mum, shiny shoes came very far down on the list and I lost the discipline along the way. One grandson, however, still has shiny shoes.

YOU'VE BEEN FRAMED

To say Dad was not a practical man would be minimising the fact. Times were hard and my parents were always inventing ways to save money. Mum had the bright idea Dad could make picture frames so they invested in a mitre board and some long pieces of wood. Dad just could not get the idea, losing his temper whilst we all laughed at the pile of very small pieces which might have made good dolls' house frames if anyone had the patience to put them together.

SOUL TO SOLE

Dad did manage to master the art of shoe mending, this through shear necessity. I can remember him in 'the shed' with an iron foot called a last on which he placed a shoe with the sole uppermost. He had a square piece of leather and a very sharp knife and cut the leather to the size of the sole. He then used tiny nails to hammer around the edge of the sole to affix it to the shoe. The heels needed a little more craftsmanship but were attached in the same manner. I still have two unanswered questions. Why did he hold the nails in his mouth? When did he realise the shoes needed mending? The second one perhaps when his socks started squelching. In later years the leather was replaced by 'Phillips Stick on Soles and Heels' affixed by foul-smelling glue.

SHARING

My sister and I shared a bedroom until I left home to be married at twenty-one. I am sure she was overjoyed to have this tiny bedroom to herself. In later years we had two single beds but initially we shared a double bed. It must have been dreadful for her, although she has no memory of this. Sad how bad things from childhood are stored and sometimes distorted; at the age of thirty-four I was discussing bed-wetting with my Mum. I said I could remember my sister wetting the bed and was shocked to find it was me! I can remember waking often on soggy linen and a rubber sheet underneath. I was obviously ashamed and had convinced myself that it was my sister's problem. Glad to say that at the present time I am not wetting the bed; as old age creeps up, who knows? As I now live alone there will be no-one else to blame!

VIRGIN THOUGHTS

My first 'sexual experience' and one which made my heart thump so much I felt everyone in the cinema could hear it, was at a showing of the 'Blue Lamp'. I think it was Dirk Bogarde who pressed his hand against the heroine's chest and said "Let me feel your ticker". I was so naïve I did not know what a ticker was but my hormones told me it was something sexy! I was really disappointed later to learn that it was the heart but the hand pressed against the bosom was real enough!

JAW BREAKERS

Mum talked about Jaw Breakers, a large type of sweet – toffee perhaps from her childhood. Both Mum and Dad were partial to Thornton's Toffee and liked Rum and Butter toffees from Woolworth's. My sister worked on Saturdays at the sweet counter. Dad was always given a little more than a 'quarter' (one quarter of an imperial pound) when he bought his Saturday ration.

Someone else's childhood memory

MODESTY

We talked about the sea and the days when everyone tried to change into their costumes with just a towel covering them. My friend remembered when she was small and seeing a man beside them whose towel blew away. Her Grandmother then in her sixties and living alone for some time, was quite taken with this vision and was sorely scolded by her son, my friend's Dad saying "For God's sake Mother". It is only now that my friend realised the real reason for the stares.

In 2004 I travelled with my sister on the Rocky Mountaineer train through Canada and here we met the wonderful Carlotta who was our tour guide

CARLOTTA FROM CANADA

Nova Scotia, Canada, a province blessed with much; beautiful landscapes, old and new history, down-home people, of course the good times and the bad times as much of the world has seen. Our country had been to war, several times but has never seen war in recent times, not since the War of 1759 on the Plains of Abraham in Quebec when what was a country was officially declared a British stronghold and finally the war of 1812 between Canada and the United States. We are still a country strong and great. A country formed in 1867 "Oh Canada. Our home and native land." Growing up in the 60s was much like most places and of course being influenced by what was going on in the US, such an exciting place to us who yearned for excitement during that new age of music, Rock and Roll. But dreams were all that was allowed as my two sisters and one brother were very much expected to share in the 'chores' of the farm on which we lived and conducted our lives from day to day.

Even 'going to town' nearby if you call three miles nearby, was exciting, especially on Saturday afternoon to see a movie matinee. Money was collected through running errands and doing chores, that is if there was any money left over for such 'luxuries'. We had a very happy life on the farm, loving, caring parents and grandmother with lots of relatives who came for weekly visits. Life was discussed around the wood stove in the kitchen. For many communities this was a place to gather for music and dance, but not for our family. Spring was coming, an eagerly awaited time after a long cold winter in Nova Scotia.

The morning started like any other day with a hearty breakfast prepared by our mother for four children and our father who had already begun his day, milking the cows and feeding the livestock on the small farm on which we lived. He would later leave for his job as a Mortician with one of the two Funeral Homes in the nearby town of Windsor. We had our usual family breakfast of oatmeal porridge, bacon, eggs, homemade toasted bread, homemade strawberry jam, finished off with a sugared doughnut and a glass of farm fresh milk. Now it was time for mother to do our hair; mine in ringlets, my sisters with braided hair. I was later to find out how I was hated for having curls.

Our brother had already left for school with his friends. After the hair does we left for school; my sister Bernice and myself. We made our way down the pathway to the road to walk the half mile to the schoolhouse. For several days the temperature had been getting warmer but there was still lots of snow along the sides of the road. We reached the boardwalk across the ditch but really couldn't judge where the boardwalk was. Down we went through the slushy snow. My sister with both legs stuck in the snow and I with one leg stuck to my hip; the other leg was on top of the snow. We could not move. The wet snow held us firm. Of course we were frightened and started to call for help. No one heard. We pushed and pulled with all our might but no luck in getting out of the mess we were in. Again we called. No one came. Finally we saw our neighbour walking down the road.
He saw the predicament we were in and returned home to get a shovel to dig us out. Soaking wet we returned to our home, changed our clothes and walked to school. I don't think our teacher quite believed our story.

1960s

Here we have stories about other people's children and some from my family

LET US PRAY

In my early twenties, before I had children, I babysat a young Irish girl of 5 years. She was really good but when I tucked her in bed she asked if we could pray as she did with her Mum. In a beautiful Irish accent she said "Can we do Hail Mary?" I am not Catholic and said it would be good if she started and I would join in if I could. I was fascinated to listen to this tiny soul praying intensely to Mary. "Can you do prayers?" she asked me. "Yes" I said but secretly praying that I wouldn't have to. "Can you do Chart?" "I don't think I know Chart" I mumbled. "Everyone knows Chart" she said angrily. "But darling, I don't think they say Chart at my Church." "Everyone knows Chart" she shouted at me and was beginning to look tearful. To pacify her I told her to start as she had done before and I would join in if I could; she started

"Our Father **Chart** in Heaven, Hello be thy Name"!

HERE COMES THE BRIDE

Our lovely dog, Bob was a Collie cross, crossed with some human genes I think. He smiled; he tried to talk and got so excited when anyone knocked at the door. Although my Mum loved him, she had a little hearing difficulty and his bark sometimes aggravated this, causing her to utter a few swearwords. Our little family, with a two year old son, visited Mum one day; the usual rapping at the door caused the dog to bark – "Buddy dog" shouted my son.

The dog's instincts were amazing. We lived on the main road and any number of buses pulled up opposite our house. Bob always knew, however, which one my sister was on, running up the stairs to look out of the front bedroom window, waiting for her to cross the road. His head would peep out from under the net curtains which would tumble down each side and across his ears, with his black nose protruding from the white lacy veil. Everyone who passed would smile and he was given the name 'Bride Dog'.

CHRISTOPHER (1969)

Chatterbox has gone to bed
His conversation fills my head
Whassis, whadat and why not mum?
Mummy, Mummy – me have some.
Don't touch the gas, put down the cat.
Now Mummy said enough of that.
Why Mum, what for, when and where,
Two year olds don't seem to care
If saucepans bang and dishes break
And cause his 'night-work' Dad to wake.
He talks and talks on endlessly
You'd think he'd stop to eat his tea.
But now he's sound asleep in bed,
His Teddy resting by his head.
Peace now reigns; it's quiet again,
And then at nearly half past ten
As quietly to his room I creep –
Chris is talking in his sleep!

1970s

EYES OF A CHILD

We were pretty hard up and it was the day before my second son was born. We had decorated the nursery within a very limited budget and prepared the crib. I went to admire the work and realised that the carpet was somewhat threadbare. I panicked; "We can't have a baby arriving to a threadbare carpet, what will it think?" Neither time nor funds to buy a new one, I spent the next two hours on my hands and knees, filling in the threads with a blue felt-tip pen so that my son, who came about five hours later, would not feel hard done by.

*see 2007

STICKY STORY

In the seventies I was lecturing my fairly young children on the dangers of drug taking and glue sniffing. "Don't do harm to yourselves, you are beautiful now and I would kill you if I found out you were doing any of these dreadful things." My youngest son, aged five went hysterical, screaming "I didn't mean to". When he calmed down he explained that as he was putting together his model plane, he had smelled the glue and was fearful I was going to kill him for doing so.

NEXT PLEASE

In the seventies our GP surgery was in an end of terrace house; the waiting room was the front room with an odd assortment of chairs placed around an old coffee table covered in out of date magazines, never sorted and a couple of tatty children's books. There may also have been a toy car under the table. The room was always full and no matter what time of year, the window was open encouraging the breeze to blow the flowery curtains and whisk away any germs intending to linger beneath 'The Haywain' on the wall. Children were easily bored and no amount of distractions could entertain them for long. It was a long wait too as our Doctor gave everyone the amount of time they needed. My eighteen month old son got louder and louder as I tried to interest him, yet again, in pictures from the magazines. Suddenly he could see the value and immense joy to be gained from reading. He took each magazine and one by one stood in front of every sick person in the room demanding that they took the book from him and commanding them to "**READ!**". I still don't know who was the more embarrassed but it was certainly not my baby boy.

I was later to work in another surgery for an equally dedicated GP; the queues and the wait were long. Children became testy once they had read and built bricks and scraped toy cars around the carpet. One lad stridently insisted that his Mum read louder to him. Mum did not seem confident in reading aloud to an audience and continued to whisper. This was not satisfactory for the child.

After rebuking him, trying to read some more and becoming slowly exasperated, Mum decided she would go to the toilet at the side of the room and stayed perhaps a little longer than usual. The young lad's next move was to hammer on the door. "Mum, have you finished?" "Mum, come out of there." "Mum I want you to read." "Mum I want a wee." Knocking became ear-splitting as did the voice of her son. He was causing a scene, Mum shouting from inside for him to be quiet which he did for a while. Everyone breathed a sigh when suddenly little man spied the notice on the door and at the top of his voice shouted "Mum, what does Wuh Cuh mean?" (WC). Mum tried to tell him from inside the room, her mumbled response barely audible. Again he shouted, louder this time and leaning on the door which suddenly flew open and a very red faced Mum shouted back 'Water Closet'.

Everyone adopted awkward mode, jointly gazing at the floor. Mum returned to her seat trying hard to avoid eye contact. She grabbed her son, placed him on her lap and everything became calm. As she walked into the surgery the boy looked at me and said in a loud voice "Water closet, what's a water closet?"

NEWBORN

Cautious steps, faltering, stumbling
Go, go arms outstretch; nothing to hold
Legs are those of a new-born foal, only more
so.
Foals know nothing about falling
They learn not to fall. They learn to run,
jump.
Don't look down! Knees bend; Forward
Enemy to the left; the right; behind.
Now, now, go – fast forward and the enemy
will retreat, move aside.
Why must I do it alone? Why will no-one help
me?
I feel so tall, yet I am small
A learner in this new life of twists and turns
pirouettes and spins.
My legs are so still, arms helpless.
No protection.
Go, go arms outstretch.
I go, I stop, I move, I stumble – reach out
into the cold empty air
For nothing
Down, down I go amongst the steely sharp
weapons zipping around, above me.
Pain.
My knee, my back, my bottom –
Wet?
Oh, will I never learn to skate.

(This is the day my eight year old son started to skate!)

P C

We lived near Clapham Junction in the sixties, did a lot of our shopping in Northcote Road, and had a number of friends from different races with different skin colours. It was a multi-racial area and this was reflected in the clothes and food on sale in the market. When my eldest son was four we moved to Morden. When he was almost five he had to go into hospital to have his tonsils out. I was shocked when recuperating at home he told me he hated black people. I went through the names of all our Black and Asian friends but he was still adamant. He had very little influences outside our home, only recently starting Nursery School and I despaired at what had caused him to feel so deeply. I questioned him again, explaining our principles about equality, "Why do you hate them?" His reply – "They give you injections!"

FIONA

Fiona was quite young when a nightmare awakened her and she crept downstairs for some comfort from her Mum. Mum was deep into a mystery thriller on TV and Fiona watched horrified as an Agatha Christie character peeled off her gloves after murdering her victim. A sharp intake of breath alerted Mum to the child behind the chair. A few weeks later Fiona watched as Mum got ready to go out, carefully adding gloves and pushing the fingers into the correct place. For a long time after Fiona was convinced her mother was a murderer.

1980s

ARM IN ARM

From when I was quite small I loved to walk
holding on to my Dad's arm. As years
passed my arm seemed to go higher on the
inside whilst his head became lower. Or did
I become taller? He would always let go of
my arm to doff his cap to neighbours coming
the other way.

RABBITS

We had a rabbit, an orphan that came with a cage and a manky bag of straw. My inquisitive son wanted to know if it was a boy or a girl. I couldn't answer and every attempt to pick up the animal became impossible as it wriggled and struggled and scratched my arms to pieces, jumping high into the air and disappearing quickly into the rose bed. After a few weeks and when I returned from work, 'Thumper' was lying in the sun, stretched to his full length and enjoying the warmth on his furry belly. When my lad came in from school I was happy to tell him that I had discovered Thumper was a boy rabbit. "How do you know Mum?" he asked. "Well he was lying in the sun, on his back, with his belly facing upwards." My son, looking amazed at me, replied "Don't be silly Mum, girl rabbits do that too!"

ACCEPTABLE

The world has changed since I was young.
Couples often live together for some time
before marrying, some never marry. My son
and his girlfriend had just bought a house
together. My granddaughter asked "How
many years do you have to live together
before you get married?" Some years earlier
my partner and I set up home together long
before we married. My nine year old niece
visited and we did a tour of the rooms; I
showed her our bedroom. "Where does
Uncle sleep? "In here, with me" I answered.
She looked puzzled and replied "I thought
only Americans did that".

HILLSBOROUGH

EE I ADD Y O (16th April 1989)

Today we're gonna thrash 'em Mam, do it
like before
Today we'll give it to 'em Mam and then we'll
give some more
I should be back by midnight Mam; we'll
have chips on the way
But if you save me dinner Mam, I'll have it
anyway

He went off in the charra with his scarf
around his neck
They called for our Tommy who just moved
down by the bec.
They sang their songs and shouted as they
went off down our street
This band of Kenny's army who we said
could not be beat

They go there very early so the lads could
see the game
They thought that seats were cissy, it just
would not be the same
They sang and cheered and chanted and on
came Kenny's lads
And the crowd was filled with pride, full of
kids and mums and dads

The whistle blew in Sheffield, back home a
mum sat down

Drank tea and ate a biccy when she got back
from the town
She thought about our Tommy, very soon to
be a dad
Of the days she had with Kevin who was
such a happy lad

She was worried about father and his
problems with his job
And the problems at the dockside where
there was an angry mob
But she laughed and thought of football
which put all his cares away
And the pride there was at Anfield now and
every Saturday

As she gazed at TV, horses suddenly a
change of scene!
There was panic, fright and terror where the
harmony had been
There were polis, kids and stretchers and a
frightened TV voice
Now poor Kenny's army had no reason to
rejoice

Her heart cried 'E I ad y o' and her voice
gave out a moan
And she knew from this day onward she
would 'ever walk alone'
From the day when Kevin went off in his reds
and with his friend -

To the day when she will see him when her life comes to an end

As I write this tale of sorrow and I think that could be me
Waiting home on Saturday evening wondering where my son could be
Another football hero, one of Kenny's faithful band
Of which there must be thousands scattered right throughout this land

I send my love out to you, bereaved mothers, wives and friends
And I hope all prayers will help you and your pain eventually mends
And I hope that when you see him, little Kevin on that day
He will still be playing football in a place not far away

I wrote this poem the day after the Hillsborough disaster and I sent it to Liverpool Football Club

ANOTHER STICKY TALE

My sister worked as a school assistant and often had to tie shoe laces for smaller children. Not wanting to be left out, one small child asked her every day to tie his shoes which were affixed by Velcro.

ANGELIC

Mary gave us her story earlier in the narrative. She didn't have children of her own but was a wonderful friend, surrogate Mum, Aunt and Grandmother, many children now in their thirties remembering her kindness and love. The last of her charges was cared for a couple of times a week whilst her Mum worked; the little child was four and Mary was in her eighties. Apart from problems with her legs, Mary was full of life and had lots of things to tell small children. Mary was tall and big built. The little girl asked Mary what happens when people die. "They go to heaven" she replied. "What do they do there?" Mary thought for a while and then said "They are angels, with white frocks and wings". The child looked puzzled, and then smiling turned to Mary and said "When you die Mary you will have to have a very big frock".

WICKED MOTHER?

My sister and her two daughters are really frightened of creepy crawlies, spiders, mice etc. possibly a lot more than most people. Dad worked late every night and the windows had to be left open for their cats to come in and out, usually accompanied by what they described as giant spiders. One child was three, the other thirteen and my sister old enough to know better! The two older family members screamed at the tiny soul, trying to get her to pick up and throw out the spider. As a result, she has severe arachnophobia. The second part of this story takes place when they were just a bit older, Dad out again, when the cat brought in a mouse. My sister disappeared and locked herself in the bathroom, leaving the children with cat and mouse. Dad arrived home to hear Mum screaming out of the bathroom window and fearing the worst for his children, rushed in leaving the car engine running. There he found the children who had rescued the mouse and shooed the cat. They tried in vain to get my sister out of the bathroom to see this sweet little thing but she would not budge until it had gone.

UN DEUX TROIS

My son was learning French. Having taken French at school some 29 years before, I decided I would help him and did so as many evenings as I could. After a few weeks I had a message from his French teacher "Could you please stop helping your son with his homework, he is beginning to sound like Inspector Clouseau".

BY THE SEA

Daddy will you please build me a castle?
With a big pond, I think he means a moat!
Will you make it big with shells and lots of water?
And Daddy – will you please buy me a boat?

Daddy smiles and digs and fetches pails of water
Which just sinks away, makes ripples in the sand;
And a teardrop joins the ripples, slowly sinking.
Little boys of four just cannot understand

Where the water goes and Daddy tries to show him
Dries the tears away and a tickle makes him smile.
To the water's edge a child runs full of laughter
The castle will be finished in a while.

Two more teardrops wet the castle, Daddy's crying
Will his castle hold against the flowing tide?
Little boys of four just cannot understand
Why a Daddy has a pain that he must hide.

So my little son I'll build your sandy fortress
And I hope that when a Daddy you will be
If your tears along the shore are sadly
flowing
Pray your castle will be stronger than the sea

I wrote this for a friend who had a young son and so many
worries. 1983

JANNI

Janni had a fantastic childhood; her parents were very adventurous and took their children around the world before they started full-time school. Janni now in her twenties has a memory of travelling to Europe on a train. Mum had been teaching her the importance of washing hands and all about germs. Janni was playing cafes with her sister and shouted loudly the disgust she felt at 'having dirty Germans all over her'; this to the amusement of the packed train but the great embarrassment of her parents. We met Janni and her family at the airport at the end of their trip, two tiny barefoot girls, much more worldly wise than less travelled kids their own age. Janni was telling a rapt audience of their travels, where they had been, what they had done and finished the saga, hands on hips with "We haven't been to China you know".

CAROLE

Carole found it hard to remember a childhood story but her daughters remembered a tale she had told them from her young life in the sixties. Carole loved music, had lots of records. Her favourite was 'These Boots were made for Walking' by Nancy Sinatra. She played it so many times, she knew all the words. It was her favourite. One day she ran to her older brother's bedroom, excited to tell him something. She was so excited she forgot to knock and there was her brother, in all his glory and showing his backside. He was so embarrassed and so angry with her that he dressed quickly, ran to her bedroom and threw all her records out of the window, using them as 'Frizbees' to see how far they would go and Nancy Sinatra was never to he heard again. Always, always knock before entering!

ALISON'S ADVENTURES

My Mum and Dad both worked full-time when my brother and I were kids but we were lucky that my grandparents (on my Dad's side) lived fairly nearby so we used to spend a lot of time with them during the summer holidays. They would either take us both out or sometimes, as my brother was a bit older, it was just me. We had a lot of fun and our outings would either be visiting different places for the day or just tagging along whilst Granny and Granddad went about their everyday lives which although sounds dull, was always an adventure.
I used to love going with Granddad to get his MOT done. I was always very impressed with the ramp that lifted Granddad's car high into the air so that we could see underneath it. I'd never seen the underneath of a car before! The other thing I used to like about his car having the MOT was when the mechanics drove it on to the wheels in the floor. Granddad's car actually travelled without moving – Magic!

I remember that in the summer they would take us for days out at the seaside. We went to Ferring and Goring and my Granny would pack a lunch for us (which I would be looking forward to eating all morning.)

There was a patch of grass between where Granddad would park the car and the beach. We would kick a ball about; fly our kites and play Frizbee and catch. We must have left really early in the morning to get there as we were always one of the first cars to arrive and we were also usually one of the last to leave in the evening. Lunchtime would eventually come around and we were rewarded with the delights of the feast that Granny had packed up for us before we had left home. Looking back now I'm not sure how they managed to get everything in the boot of the car along with all our toys, chairs, blankets, towels, buckets and spades. The best part of Granny's feast was the fruit cake that she made in preparation for our days out. I've never since tasted anything quite as good. It was always wrapped in greaseproof paper and the smell would make your mouth water. I can taste it now…mmm delicious!

On the not-so-sunny days we would go to National Trust land or properties. One of the trips that still makes me chuckle was a visit to Batemans with my Grandparents and their friend Pat. My brother was not with us on the trip, so I sat in the back with Pat on the journey and she shared around her Soft mints (minty moo moo's as she called them).

We walked around the grounds and came across a summerhouse. Pat liked to play along with games that we would both think up. We pretended that Granny and Granddad were Lord and Lady of a stately home and Pat was a friend that they had invited over for afternoon tea. I played the part of their maid and set about asking them what they would like to eat and drink. My Granny and Granddad asked if they could have some scones and a cream tea each. I then went to take Pat's order. She asked for 'an aperitif'. I couldn't quite work out what she'd asked for so asked for her to repeat her order; she did and I had heard it as she had said the first time. I replied "Why do you want a pair of teeth when you have a perfectly good pair of your own?" I didn't know what an aperitif was and so misunderstood what she'd said. I wasn't sure why they were all falling about with laughter. After a while they regained enough composure to explain their amusement. We laughed all the way home!

OLD JIM

Jim was born in 1910 and died in March 2001. He was well known in the area as he had a steam engine which he would put on to a trailer and take to fairs all over the country. He was a real character; always wore his cap at a jaunty angle and it wasn't for many years that I discovered he was almost bald. He would sit for hours watching my husband milling, grinding and welding and they had many wonderful conversations about engineering feats and their combined crafting skills. Jim had lived in Morden and Sutton all his life and remembered this suburban area before there were houses. We lived on Stonecot Hill, the houses built on the site of Stonecot Hall that had burnt down in the late twenties. Beside the hall was a pond where horses were washed and a poultry farm owned by Miss Garratt who also owned shops and it is said she liked to gamble. The poultry farm was owned by Miss Taylor who won prizes at Crystal Palace for her Buff Orpingtons. Jim said she always wore boots that were covered in chicken muck. There was a woman named Laura White whom everyone called Madam White.

Jim said "Madam White was a funny old dear, you could play football on the meadow if you asked her but if you played without asking she would call the police". Jim and his engine gave such pleasure to many children (and grown up children). In 1993 I wrote this poem for him. He never mentioned it but when we went to his funeral the poem was read. Jim had kept it with his Will; I think he must have appreciated it.

JIM

Pistons and pumps and pleasing some people
He walks down the road with his cap at a tilt
He goes out quite early on Saturdays and Sundays
With his car and a trailer and an engine he built

Gleaming and steaming and blowing with pleasure
Old Mr Watt would smile with great pride
Magnificent, masterpiece, truly a treasure
I wonder what it is made of inside

Is it coal boils the water which in turn makes the steam?
Can he tune it and tweak it, make it go like a dream?

Jim's in his eighties still looks a lad
As he did in his thirties when he first was a dad
He knows what he's doing when he's off to a fair,
There are hundreds of Jims, all ages everywhere

But they don't have an engine to polish and clean
They don't have the knowledge to build one
At the end of a rally when Jim's boiler they've seen
They admire the work the 'old boy's' done

There are so many Jims in so many places
An enthusiast spreads so much joy
Which is seen in the gleam on hundreds of faces
Which are mirrored in the shine of this 'toy'

So keep polishing and oiling, fine tuning the thing
Till the day when your steam finally goes
And the memory of Jim and the joys that you bring
Will ever be there at the shows.

October 1993

143

Now we enter the world of Grandchildren; a magical world in which I am privileged to be.

SANTA

We were singing Christmas songs in the car with three of our granddaughters, the youngest of whom was not too happy about an old man with a beard coming down their chimney. Granddad and I decided to sing the one about Mummy kissing Santa Claus. The youngest one started screaming "Stop singing".

The middle one most affronted shouted "My Mum did not kiss Santa Claus". The eldest, six years old asked "Is that the end?" I told her yes but asked why she wanted to know. "I was waiting for the part when they take off their clothes." TV or peer influence?

READING AGE?

My 4 year old granddaughter was being naughty, pulling plants out of a pot which I asked her not to do. She gave me the plant label. "What does this say Nan?" I replied "It says please put this back immediately". She took it, looked at the label and replied "No it doesn't, it says put it back in a minute".

OLD BARBIE DOLL

My granddaughter had a pink frieze with Barbie Doll heads around her bedroom. She was counting them when she asked "How old are you Nan?" "Fifty-nine" I replied. She looked amazed and said "That's enough Barbies to go round my room, S's room, L's room, down the stairs, round the hall and into the kitchen".

CONCEPTS

Explaining the meaning of 'today' is fine but how do you explain other similar words - yesterday, tomorrow, last night? Tomorrow never comes does it? S was trying to explain to me something that happened a few days ago. "Not tonight Nan but the other tonight." At the same time P was trying to explain something she had done yesterday at school that had been 'very goodly'.

BAA BAA

We were travelling through inner city London, passing Neasden on a wet and grey November day; trains, houses, more houses and rain. My 5 year old granddaughter looked out of the window and said "Those poor sheep will get their cotton wet". When we asked her where she had seen sheep she told us she hadn't but was just thinking about sheep.

TERRIBLE TWOS

Parents please remember that two year-olds cannot yet reason and only know their own world. They are not yet able to put themselves into another's shoes and see another point of view. I know a number of adults who can't do that either!

THE FARM

A group of five year olds watched two goats being born at the farm. One asked the assembled crowd if she had been born in a rucksack!

2 YEARS, MY EXPERIENCE – LEDA FROM CHILE

Well everything, started two years ago and, well, all I can say about my journey to England it's that everything was wonderful, not how I expect it, but it was okay anyways. In this document I'll write how did I felt since when my Dad told me we were going to England, the change that I had there in that country and when I came back to my country. How was my experience and how did I felt and everything.

In two years everything could change, the way I thought about the world, the way my feelings were, the way I treated or how my relationship with my parents etc. was. It was 2 years ago I remember well, I'm going to talk about how I was before I came to England and well I was in year 6. In my country you have a president that represent your year in different classes of different years, and that was me, I was the president of my year and I could say I think I was one of the popular of my year :S I guess because, just like I did in England and I still do here, it talk a LOT.

I don't know why, but I just love talking to everyone, don't matter how they are, or where did they come from, I love talking to all the persons I met ☺

So it was in October, oh yes! LOL ☺   My Dad came up to my room and called my sisters (my Mum was with him) so he told us that we were going on travel to Europe. I asked him where? And he was like: England! So I was like wow really? How, when? I was so excited on that moment, that I didn't knew what to say, all I knew was, that I will be very far away from where I should be (home). I'll have to speak another language different to my one, but it would be another adventure in my life so all I had to do was face it.

In November I told all my friends that I'll do a party in my house because I might not see them in 2 years, so everything was going OK (at that moment I had 12 years old) and I did my party :D. So it was the time went so far those 3 months, it was now ending December, my family and I was doing the invitations for New Year eve because we were going to do a party, my family and I love doing party and going to parties because it's a very common thing.

Oh well when I came to England it was snowing ☺ it was so beautiful seeing the snowing falling down, it wasn't usual to me to see snow in the city. In my country Chile, we have everything: Deserts, Forests, Sea (the Pacific Ocean) Mountains, Cities (but the snow is just on the mountains no in the cities) etc. My country actually has EVERYTHING. The only bad thing is that it doesn't have that much history because we just have 200 years of history written. But I believe we have much more, because there was a news that said in Chile some Scientifics found a mommy that it has more years than the mommies in Egypt. So somehow I just think South America has more years than others countries in Europe or even Asia!

But, oh well, since I got to England the way of how I saw the world was different because one of the things Chile needs, it's got more culture. My country isn't that clean but it is because the own people don't want it to be cleaner... But in England if you dare to throw something to the street or anywhere else except some bin, there would be a penalty to the person who isn't obeying the law. I think some cities could be so beautiful but they just need to be cleaner, that's all ☺.

Also the thing I most love of England is how can that country have so many different cultures and races, I would love my country to be like that.

So, when I get to a secondary school in England, called St Mary's Catholic High school, they accept me easily but how I didn't speak proper English. I remember that a girl used to do bullying against me and I didn't like it at all, but bullying its everywhere, in all the school there is a person who annoys everyone. With the time I learned quickly English word, and how to express myself etc. I made a lot of friends and I really loved the time I spend with them. I made friends from all over the world and that's the coolest thing ever because I never thought I could do that one day. I also learned how was the way of living in different countries, different foods, everything. It is easy to me make a lot of friends but to trust them and make the friendship longer, that's difficult, even if I'm in Chile. I am still in contact with many friends that I made in England and I would love to meet them again in life....

I don't want to make this very longer so I'll be ending this with how people respect other people, doesn't caring how they are or where they come from.

I'm not saying England it's the best country, everyone have bad things and good things, but I'm glad and thankful for having the luck to stay in England for 2 years, learning the language and meeting different people from different countries, with different point of view and opinions.

Yours sincerely, Leda Llancaman

I met Leda, her sisters and her parents through a Spanish Club in Croydon. When they returned to Chile, they agreed to send me their stories. Leda was born in 1997, Rayen in 2001 and Dane in 2002. They went back to Chile in January 2012. I have not edited their stories because I am very proud to read their written English.

2000s

DANE FROM CHILE

In October 3rd, when our father told us we were going to England I asked this:

"What is England?" and Rayen was like this:

After that we learned the numbers from 0 to 1000 before going to England . At that time we already knew what was England, where it was and that it belonged to Europe. Before being in England I imagined that it was exactly like Chile and that all the other countries were the same. Even if my parents explained me more, I didn't understand all of it. Also we didn't know what Great Britain was but when we got there we understand all written recently. When we got to England and the plane was landing I looked down and there was ice! Then a car came for us and we were going to Croydon it started snowing.

When we got to the hotel of Croydon the city was covered in snow! Afterwards, when we already had a house, we started to move things to have more space. We started to go to the car boots where you could buy good things in an excellent price. Now my Mum sometimes is frustrated because she didn't bring all the things we bought. Here in Chile there aren't much beautiful things like there were in England.

I was the last one to be registered in a school. When entered one, all my classmates talked to me but the problem was that I didn't understand them. ☺. Only one girl was bad with me, when it was the second break time I played with a boy that talked Spanish so I played with him but in the first one there was a girl that always (in the first week) bullied me but the good thing was that one week after she left the school ☺. Now that I'm in fourth grade in Chile, my English teacher teaches me what I learned in England in the first week. I still hope that my classmates learn English because it would really help them find a good job when they grow up. Some of my classmates ask me how to say things but only one asked me how to say a dirty word ☹.

The things that I most missed when I was in England were the artichoke, water melon, trencito chocolate and sane-nuss chocolate. The places that I missed going to the beach, the swimming pool and some cool games near the beach. The difference between Chile and England were that there were foxes, they were shy but I loved to see them, sometimes even hided and followed them. Only once I saw a fox with a gigantic fish in its mouth. There were a lot of news that said they were dangerous If they were really hungry.

Other difference was that there weren't many bars in the houses because in England they don't steal that much like in Chile. Even though there weren't many robs, England was covered in cameras. Once when I went to a castle there was a camera hidden in the mouth of a statue in Warwick Castle

By Dane Iren Llancaman Torres

RAYEN FROM CHILE

My life in Chile was going to school and in school we bring our bag with full of books, notebooks, pencils. Sometimes they ask for materials which we have to buy and then bring them to school. They give homework like one time at a day or test (well they advise 1, 2 or one month before the test) every day to school. If you did not have 4 classes with good notes, you have to repeat year.

In England (in the primaries) they have the books in school, the pencils, and in our bag we just bring our reading book and a book but some children want to bring their own pencils. And some schools they give homework at Friday. In nursery and from year 1 to 5 there was no test, but in year 6, before the end of the year, they do the SIMCE (test including math, literacy and science) for knowing if you have the knowledge to pass to secondary.

In Chile we celebrate Christmas, Pacific ware and police day, Easter day, Mum's day, Children day, the women's day, the worker day, Fiestas Patrias. In England you celebrate Christmas, St George, St Patrick, Easter day, the worker day.

Before I left Chile, in the last week of September (in 2009) I was a normal girl just like any Chilean girl going to school every day and when I grow up decide her future, but in the first week of October, I didn't know that it was going to change. "Girls, in my job they tell me that we got a trip to England" my Dad says. "What's that" My little sister ask (Dane) and he explain what was it and that we need to go, well we did not get that upset, we just get a little bit surprise.
The next year we have to go, just before that Leda make a party in Friday, Dane in Saturday and me in Sunday.

I left my home in Valparaiso, the next day my family and I go to my Grandma's house in Quilpue where the next day we leave and get up in the plane said goodbye to our beautiful Chile. I have never ever get in a plane so my first thought was it will be great, well it was like that but all the time I spend watch movies, listen to music or play games because in the plane, when someone sit in the front of themselves, this is where you can do anything you want. When I got out of the plane it was cold, outside there was a lot of snow, but when we go through the city, there was snowing so fast and it was full of it. That first winter my sisters and I made a snowman in our backyard.

It was difficult to learn English especially for me because I am not much communicated. I did not make actually friends but before 6 months that we need to go I make 4 friends where I am still in contact with them.

Rayen Alejandra Llancaman Sepulveda

SPECIAL EYES

After a short eye test at school, L came home with a note to visit the Optician. Dad asked her about the eye examination. Her reply, "I couldn't read the bottom lines but how could I, they made them too small."

MUST TRY HARDER

"Do you go to work Nan?" my granddaughter asked. "I work on Tuesdays." (I did not want to go into explanations about retirement and voluntary work which I felt would complicate things for a six year old.) Her reply – "Nan you will have to learn more".

MORE PRAYERS

S aged six had just joined Girls' Brigade and showed me how I must pray. This became the most beautiful mixture of Christian hands together, a yoga position and a little bit of Disney's Pocahontas.

ASHES TO ASHES

We had lost our beautiful cat in April 2001; he was cremated and remained in a tiny blue pot, buried just below the surface at the bottom of the garden. The girls always talked about him as they did Granddad who had died in November the same year. In the summer of 2003 the older girls' curiosity got the better of them. "Can we see where he is buried?" one asked. I lifted the stone and showed them the top of the little blue urn. The youngest (5), with a puzzled look, scanned the remainder of the garden. "What is it darling?" I asked. "Where is Granddad?"

INBETWEEN

My granddaughter and her friend ran out of school excited and anxious to break the news. The over-extended mannerisms copied from TV stars and Soap Queens were employed to describe the new playground romance. "We knew she fancied him because she told us and this morning he kissed her hand and oh Nanny what do you think?" I was about to utter a completely inadequate sentence when the outburst continued; "and Zoe just told us she had been told by Natasha that she had seen them kissing on the lips!" More gesticulations, more feminine turning of the head and widening of the eyes showed me that my little Granddaughter was growing up.

Two hours later as I prepared to go home, I searched the house for her to say goodbye. Where did I find her? Camped under her bed playing with her dolls!

BULLIED

I stood in the playground and watched the
line
They were singing and dancing, the name
was mine
They laughed and they jeered, I was only ten
Then they shouted and hit me and laughed
again
I cried inside, I died inside

Alone in the playground I watched the line
They chanted and bellowed, the name was
mine
'Old fatty Falkner' was what I heard
No-one would help me, I said not a word but
I cried inside, I died inside

At the age of eleven, another school
'A little more subtle' the bullying rule
Nobody knew except them and me
And it's only now that I can feel free from
The crying inside and the dying inside

(Written at 61 years)

DOG'S BREAKFAST

Daddy was talking to me about his friend
who had just bought a Chocolate Labrador.
"Will it melt?" his daughter asked.

LOST PROPERTY

Two years after my husband died, the
grandchildren were rummaging in the
bedroom drawers. One of the children found
his watch and rushed to show it to the
others. The smallest child gasped and said
"Oh no, Granddad left his things behind".

MONEY, MONEY, MONEY

J aged three had a photo session and was brilliant, the photographer suggesting a modelling career. Her Mum was recounting the tale and I said "If you did you could keep the money in trust for her". J looked at me and said "Oh no, Bibby, I have a purse!"

SONG OF LIFE

My five year old granddaughter sang me a song over the telephone. It went on for a long time and was completely spontaneous, all the words coming out in tune but making no sense whatsoever. When she had finished I said "That was really lovely". She came back quickly with "Adults don't know that song".

WHAT A VIEW!

One of my Granddaughters and I took a trip on the Millennium Wheel by the Thames at Waterloo. There was another small child beside her who saw as far as Crystal Palace. "You can see Paris" she said. R replied "I can see the whole world". Well, it was her whole world at that time.

WEARING WELL?

My niece was talking to her three year old daughter about age. J said to her Mum "Bibby's not old, she goes to work". The next day it was my birthday. "How old is Bibby?" she asked. "Sixty four" said Mum. J's reply "Sixty four; MY GOD!"

TEACHER SAID

My Granddaughter had biology lessons at school and wanted to name all the parts of the body. Without hesitation she went through them all, ending with the large intesticle and the small intesticle

WHEN I GROW UP

One of the girlies was brushing another's hair. P looked at me and said "S wants to be a musician when she grows up". "Lovely, what instrument will she play" I asked? "No she wants to do massages and faces" was the reply. Oh – a beautician!

HOW TO EXPLAIN

It is so hard to try to explain death to small children. Two years after my husband's death my youngest Granddaughter telephoned me to ask if he was still dead; oh how I prayed for the right words to say.

COMPLIMENT

About nine months after my birthday my Granddaughter called to say "I love you so much Nanny I drawed you a birthday cake". I realised that at the age of five, birthdays are probably the most special thing and this was the best way to say I love you.

COMING AND GOING

I watched you go away from me as first you
took a stride
Then to see you walk by him, hand in hand,
side by side
Three years you went from tiny babe, a
beauty to behold
The child and man so great to see, a lovely
story told

The man adored, the child loved him,
together such a team
She taught him how to laugh and love; he
showed her how to dream
So many firsts this man and girl, trains, and
sea and shows
Will she remember, we must see, no-one
really knows

One day this man was ill and died, the child
was so bereft
Not knowing where her love had gone, the
reason why he left
But Granddad has a Grandma here to laugh
and play and dance
To help this child remember him and have
another chance

To grow and love and teach a world of very special ways

To share the joy of love from him the pleasure of those days
When first we watched you learn to walk to laugh to run and stride

And though we love the time we have, we miss him deep inside

ENCHANTING

The three girls found a CD of Buddhist Bells and Chants and wanted to hear it. After about a minute the youngest two lost interest but the eldest Granddaughter, being more sophisticated, wanted to hear the whole of the disc; another five minutes passed with the same music and although looking extremely bored, she casually asked if there were any other pop songs on the album

OFF WITH HER HEAD!

We went to Hampton Court Palace and R aged eight, ran everywhere; up and down stairs 3 at a time, with Nan trailing and puffing behind. In the Great Hall she stood entranced as a 'Tudor Lady' spoke to My Ladies and My Gentleman about her life in this wonderful place. Suddenly R tugged at my sleeve "Nan, I know that woman!" "How darling" I replied? "She used to have her head chopped off." History lessons paid off then.

A beautiful Lebanese family I met in Egypt

PEACE BUT WHEN?

The history of Lebanon is almost as old as man itself and the country has been dominated at various points by many aggressors. In 2004 on a trip to Egypt, I was privileged to meet a beautiful Lebanese family – Mum and Dad, four daughters and a son. These young people were small in the time of the dreadful Civil War in the 70s and 80s. Mum told us some terrible stories of their endeavours to survive and keep the children safe. They had lost homes and businesses on many occasions. One night Dad said that once again they had to move immediately. Mum piled the children into an old van and Dad went off in their car. After a short while they came across a road block; Mum tried to stop the van and the brakes failed. She was terrified that if she did not stop at all the van would be fired on without question and she and all the children would be killed or injured. She quickly turned off the engine and pulled on the handbrake stopping just in time for safety.

I was planning to visit Lebanon when the country was invaded by Israel following the capture of some Israeli soldiers. I called my friends; no reply at their house but managed to get hold of them on a mobile phone. They were fleeing, once again, to Beirut. They stayed for a few days and then again fleeing to Jordan and eventually back to Egypt. They are home again now; their house is still standing, no windows, lots of dust and mice.

Whilst writing this there is still a period of unrest in that country; yesterday I saw a Lebanese father on TV; his statement "I promised my children they would not go through what I did in my youth. I feel as if I have let them down." Haven't we all let them down?

More grandchildren – not all of them mine!

SUPERGRAN

Gran was amazing. She could make boats from boxes; cars from cardboard and she could make a 7 year old birthday boy laugh – a lot. She always put some money inside his cards. It was her sixty-fifth birthday and the little lad went shopping with Dad for her present. It was difficult to persuade him that she would not be able to manage a skate board to travel alongside him on his scooter. Eventually he decided on a soft toy but secretly gave her a card he had written inside which he had affixed 6 various small coins, from his piggy bank.

OUT OF THE MOUTHS

Although the youngest contributor P born in 2007 is not old enough to recount the tale herself, it must be included. This little soul, just learning to say Daddy, Mummy etc. was asked to say goodbye as Daddy was going out. "Football?" she asked in a voice which sounded rather like Mummy's and a little disgruntled!

DEPTHS

I needed a plumber but the job was too small for anyone to be interested. I mentioned this to P's Mummy. "Perhaps Peter next door can help. I'll ask him." Two days later P asked me "Has Peter plumbed you yet?"

COMICAL

There was an article in the Daily Express about an award Ps Nanny had been given. P ran to Mummy "Mummy, Mummy – Nanny's picture is in a comic!"

DISCO

Today P said "old ladies cannot go to discos". I asked if I could go – "No Nanny you are old because you are crinkly all over". This was on the same day as my great-niece told her Grandma that she looked like a little elf!

BLASPHEMY

H, only just talking, dropped his car and shouted "Sake". Dad was often heard to shout "For goodness sake", or something like that!

Thank you lovely children for all the smiles – I am awaiting more from the younger family members.

VOCABULARY

These are childhood words gathered from various sources

- "It's behind the radiogator" (radiator).

- "I've shinniffed (finished) my dinner."

- "Bufferflies" or "Flufferflies"

- "Zoe has picking pox."

- "Nan, do you wear a giraffe"? (bra)

- "My Nan and Granddad aren't old; they don't have lines on their faces. My teacher is old."

- "How are you today darling?" "I'm all K thank you."

- "Mum, we did Country Dancing at school today – showing vests!!"

- "Nan, why don't you have proper hands?"

- "Auntie J has stripes on her face."

- Mum was insistent that P should not have coca cola. P's reply "God said coke is good for you".

- S talking about the Teletubbies – "One of them is a girl and the other one is two boys".

- "Don't go through the gate Nan it's a very fizzy road".

- P trying to brush my spray-covered hair said "Oh Nanny, you have such crusty hair".

- "Mum, this T shirt's scustin."

- "Dad I have just seen an airocopter."

- "My Granddad is so clever, he can make things misappear."

- Every book one of my granddaughters reads, starts "One a ponna tie". I remember her Uncle's stories commenced "One a wassa time."

- Little girl of three pretending to read Cinderella, turns the page and says "Oh God Fairy Mother".

- Daddy washed the girls' hair in 'Head and Shoulders'. One of them asked in a very serious tone if there was one called 'Knees and Toes'.

- S was telling Dad about someone she had seen on TV who was 'nice' and 'decent'. Dad was surprised at the use of the word decent. S looked at him and said "I don't know why I said decent, I don't know what it means".

- R and I went shopping "Are we going to Marks and Spensive?"

- L watched an old James Bond film with her Dad. "Is it very old Dad?" "Why?" Dad asked. "They have old settees" she replied.

- I heard an ornament fall; silence for a while and then "It was by accident not by purpose".

- R suffering hearing effects after a cold asked me to read "Captain Brainstorm" (Jack and the Beanstalk).

- 'N is for envelope'.

- J swimming each week with her Dad uses 'gogglers' and a 'floater'.

- Asking if the Wicked Queen in Snow White was a witch I was rebuked; "Don't say that word, its rude".

- The robber was 'underested'.

- "Nanny you look wunnerful and faberlus today and you are a good driver with your wobbly arms"; (bingo bat wings).

- "Nan, you have very old eyelids."

- R was excited to tell me she had been to the cinema where she saw "The Chemicals of Narnia

- Following a recent visit to London R told me how much she enjoyed 'The Infernal War Museum'. Never a truer word!

- I am 69 and trying to learn Spanish – P is 2 and trying to learn English! I am totally inhibited and analyse everything. P is the opposite and it is fascinating to watch her learn. Her latest and wonderful new words: 'Candle Floss' and 'Very excycle'.

What joy to listen to this emerging language. (Her brother H is now learning English and I am still trying to learn Spanish.)

- Nanny, do you like folomingos? They are pink.

- If it is hot Nanny you must get a van. If you don't have one you can get one from Christmas.

REGRETS AND DIFFICULTIES

Some of the people asked found it extremely difficult to recall childhood memories, having unresolved problems from that time. One of these dear women, again eighty plus, remembers living in occupied Holland when she was always very frightened, but remembers with a smile the time when walking in a line to school they crossed a frozen lake singing and skating to 'Hi Ho, Hi Ho'.

One of the saddest stories was from a friend in Indonesia whom I had met in Bali where he was a guide. He said that although he appreciated his childhood, he did not wish to recall it as it was so sad. His mother had died when he was two months old and the responsibility for his care fell to his aunt, a very young girl and his father. He was taken from one nursing mother to another as there was no money to get milk. They were living in a very poor area. The rest remains within his memory. Life is still very hard in Bali where they have been plagued with bombs and other terrors which has reduced the number of tourists.

The following pictures are of Nell's or her husband's relatives. Possibly two Aunts, an Uncle and Grandmother – Nain Penrhos

Nell with her friends from college, aged 19

Nell told me she was aged about 16. The dress was
Shantung silk with a navy blue bow at the back

Nell with her family – Mam, Mary, Nell, John and
Margaret, during the Great War 1914-1918

My Dad Leonard Vincent Hayman Falkner, as a boy soldier at The Duke of York Military School in Dover. I think he must have been about 10 at the end of the Great War

1940 Maureen's Mother Ida Hewett and Mrs Ricardo,
Dutch refugee, whose family shared their house

Mr Ricardo in Maureen's back garden. He was a
Manager of Shell Oil Amsterdam. He and his wife left
on the last ship out of Holland.

Maureen with Mr Fontain, Dutch Banker's son learning English – 1939

1939 – The Strawsons from Streatham whose house
had been bombed. They lodged with Maureen's family
for a while and then moved to Reigate

This postcard is of Lower Kingswood Village in the
1930s

196

Francesco Camera, Italian sailor aged 29/30 on s/s Alberto de Giussano which sank during World War 2. Prisoner in Serbia repatriated to Italy in 1945 thanks to the Partesan movement

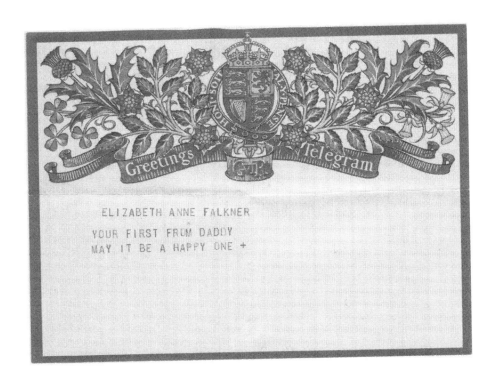

ELIZABETH ANNE FALKNER
YOUR FIRST FROM DADDY
MAY IT BE A HAPPY ONE +

Telegram from my Dad Christmas 1940

I have no photos of my beautiful Mum, Annie as a child;
this one I love – Mum and me in 1941

Another photo of my lovely Mum Annie together with my little sister Doris - 1944

Doris and me - 1945

A hand-made birthday card, January 1944

Victory Party in Rochester in 1945 – Elizabeth with arms folded; sister Doris trying to get Mum's attention!

Dad, Doris and me on the sea front, St Helier, Jersey
1952

Nanny and P just back from the park!

We are given one blessing, love, which cannot be taken away from us. Only love and all the joys will be yours, the sky, the trees, people and even yourself.

Leo Tolstoy

May peace prevail upon Earth *(Tibetan*

Prayer)

Printed in Great Britain
by Amazon